THE LYLE ANTIQUES & THEIR VALUES

AMERICANA

Compiled by Anthony Curtis

While every care has been taken in the compiling of information contained in this volume the publishers cannot accept any liability for loss, financial or otherwise, incurred by reliance placed on the information herein.

All prices quoted in this book are obtained from a variety of auctions in various countries and are converted to dollars at the rate of exchange prevalent at the time of sale.

The words "Lyle Publications" and the "Silhouette" design are registered trademarks belonging to Coward-McCann, Inc.

Copyright © 1983 by Voorhoede Publicaties B.V.
No part of this book (issue) may be reproduced in any form by print, photoprint, microfilm or any other means without written permission from the publisher unless for review purposes.

Library of Congress Cataloging in Publication Data

Curtis, Tony
  Americana.

  (The Lyle antiques and their values)
  Includes index.
  1. Americana—Collectibles—Prices.   I. Title.
II. Series.
NK805.C87   1983   745.1'0973'075   83-740
ISBN 0-698-11239-3 (Coward-McCann)

Printed in the United States of America
Distributed in the United States by Coward-McCann, Inc.,
200 Madison Avenue, New York, N.Y. 10016

INTRODUCTION

This book is one of a series specially devised to aid the busy professional dealer in his everyday trading. It will also prove to be of great value to all collectors and those with goods to sell, for it is crammed with illustrations, brief descriptions and valuations of hundreds of antiques.

Every effort has been made to ensure that each specialised volume contains the widest possible variety of goods in its particular category though the greatest emphasis is placed on the middle bracket of trade goods rather than on those once-in-a-lifetime museum pieces whose values are of academic rather than practical interest to the vast majority of dealers and collectors.

This policy has been followed as a direct consequence of requests from dealers who sensibly realise that, no matter how comprehensive their knowledge, there is always a need for reliable, up-to-date reference works for identification and valuation purposes.

When using your Antiques and their Values Book to assess the worth of goods, please bear in mind that it would be impossible to place upon any item a precise value which would hold good under all circumstances. No antique has an exactly calculable value; its price is always the result of a compromise reached between buyer and seller, and questions of condition, local demand and the business acumen of the parties involved in a sale are all factors which affect the assessment of an object's 'worth' in terms of hard cash.

In the final analysis, however, such factors cancel out when large numbers of sales are taken into account by an experienced valuer, and it is possible to arrive at a surprisingly accurate assessment of current values of antiques; an assessment which may be taken confidently to be a fair indication of the worth of an object and which provides a reliable basis for negotiation.

Throughout this book, objects are grouped under category headings and, to expedite reference, they progress in price order within their own categories. Where the description states 'one of a pair' the value given is that for the pair sold as such.

CONTENTS

American Indianware 8	Windsor Chairs. 72
Amusement Machines. 14	Chests. 74
Boxes 16	Chest of Drawers 76
Bronze 20	Chests on Chests. 82
Carved Wood 24	China Cabinets. 83
Chandeliers 30	Cupboards. 84
China 32	Desks 88
Clocks. 38	Highboys. 96
Clock Sets 38	Lowboys. 100
Longcase Clocks 40	Secretaire Bookcases 102
Mantel Clocks 42	Settees & Sofas. 104
Wall Clocks 44	Sideboards. 108
Watches 47	Stands 112
Copper & Brass 48	Stools. 116
Dolls. 50	Suites 117
Dolls' Houses 51	Tables. 123
Furniture. 52	Card Tables. 128
Beds. 52	Consol Tables 131
Bookcases 54	Dressing Tables 132
Cabinets 55	Drop-Leaf Tables 133
Candlestands 56	Pembroke Tables 136
Chairs. 58	Tavern Tables 138
Armchairs. 58	Tea Teables. 139
Ladder Back Chairs. 64	Work Tables 141
Rocking Chairs 65	Glass. 142
Side Chairs 66	Bottles 142

Bowls 144	Pewter. 204
Candlesticks. 148	Photographs 206
Decanters 150	Pianos 210
Dishes 151	Pictures 211
Jugs 152	Quilts 212
Miscellaneous 154	Samplers 218
Vases 156	Scrimshaw 220
Windows 162	Screens 222
Wine Glasses 163	Signs 223
Gramophones 164	Silver 224
Instruments 166	Bowls 224
Iron & Tin 168	Candlesticks. 225
Jewelry 170	Centerpieces 226
Juke Boxes 172	Compotes 226
Lamp Shades 173	Cups 227
Lamps 174	Dishes 228
Floor Lamps 180	Flatware 230
Tiffany Lamps 182	Jugs 232
Lanterns 186	Miscellaneous 234
Marble & Stone 188	Teapots 235
Miniature Furniture 189	Teasets 236
Mirrors 190	Trays 242
Miscellaneous 194	Tureens 242
Money Banks 196	Vases 243
Musical Boxes 200	Toys 244
Organs 202	Weathervanes 248

AMERICANA

AMERICAN INDIANWARE

One of a pair of Indian women's gauntlets with floral designs in colored beads. $200

20th century Indian eagle feather bonnet with bead work band. $200

Indian hide wedding dress painted with warriors and buffalo. $250

Plains Indian beadwork on doeskin leggings and moccasins. $300

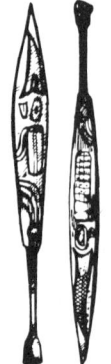

A pair of North American Indian carved wooden paddles, 46in. long. $330

North American Athapaskan Indian beaded velvet cap. $330

North American Indian tomahawk pipe with iron blade. $350

AMERICANA

AMERICAN INDIANWARE

Indian beadwork pouch with floral decoration. $375

A pair of North American Indian carved wooden paddles, 35in. long. $385

A North American Indian figure of an officer wearing a long coat with epaulettes, 10in. high. $440

Blackfoot painted parfleche, folded like a huge envelope to form a carrying case, 30in. long. $600

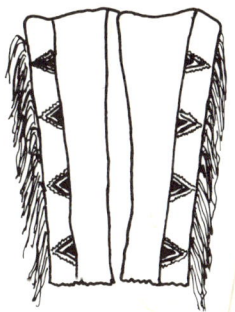

Pair of Sioux buckskin leggings, decorated with beads and fringes. $600

North American Athapaskan Indian softskin embroidered jacket. $770

AMERICANA

AMERICAN INDIANWARE

Cree needle case of felt with silk lining, outside decorated with porcupine quillwork, 5½in. long. $1,000

19th century American Plains Indian buckskin jacket, circa 1880. $1,055

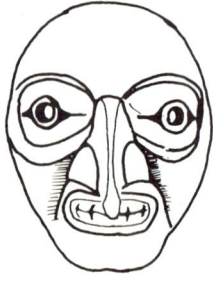

Tlingit mask representing a hawk. $1,430

Late 19th century Sioux eagle feather bonnet. $1,500

North American Sioux breastplate section, 35in. long. $1,500

A Sioux Indian hide jacket decorated with geometric motif beadwork. $1,580

AMERICANA

AMERICAN INDIANWARE

Nootka raven rattle, unusual for having a curved handle, 12in. long. $1,980

American Indian soft sole moccasins from the Eastern Great Lakes. $2,250

Pair of American Plains Indian hide and quillwork moccasins, 9½in. long. $3,040

Northern Plains Indian wood club with a gunstock like terminal inset with traces of horsehair, 32in. long. $3,040

An American North West totem pole, 13½ft. high. $3,100

A rare Red Indian ceremonial rattle filled with pebbles. $3,300

A fine and rare North West coast Indian totem pole of carved wood, 6ft. high. $3,850

AMERICANA

AMERICAN INDIANWARE

A food bowl made by the Haida Indians of Western Canada, made in the form of a mythical whale-type creature eating a man. $4,400

North American Indian carved wooden rattle, 1ft. long. $6,360

Fine American Indian Eastern Woodlands club of slender curving gunstock type, 28½in. long. $7,490

A child's rattle in the form of a round mask. $7,700

A child's rattle in the form of a stylized raven, 13½in. $9,350

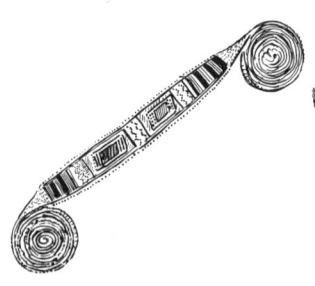

An Eastern Great Lakes burden strap composed of a long narrow strip of braided hemp. $14,000

Teton Dakota deerskin shirt bordered with beadwork. $15,000

AMERICANA

AMERICAN INDIANWARE

Tlingit circular wood face mask, 10in. diam. $26,400

An Eastern Great Lakes red cloth cloak decorated on the bottom half with a horizontal linear pattern in yellow, olive green and pale blue. $45,000

Superb Tlingit wood frontlet head-dress, 7½in. high. $49,500

Tongass wood mask, 10in. high, from the Cape Fox area. $55,000

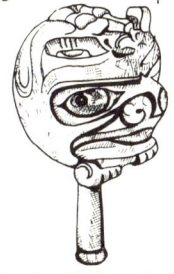

North American Haida rattle, 26.5cm. long, in carved and colored wood. $88,000

Tongass wood mask with winking eyes, 9in. high. $100,000

AMERICANA

AMUSEMENT MACHINES

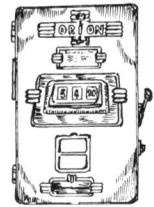

Orion one-armed bandit, circa 1960, 2ft.4in. high. $100

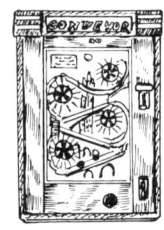

Conveyor amusement machine, 3ft. high, 1945-50. $145

American 'Twenty-one' gambling machine in cast alloy and oak casing, circa 1930, 13½in. wide. $210

Zodiac fortune teller, coin-operated machine, circa 1940, 24½in. high. $235

Sega bell fruit machine in full working condition. $280

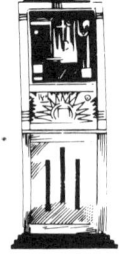

American jewel box crane penny-in-the-slot amusement machine by Buckley & Co., circa 1935, 70½in. high. $310

Auto-stereoscope in oak casing with viewer and coin slot at top, circa 1930, 22½in. high. $320

American merchantman crane amusement machine by Exhibit Supply Co., circa 1960. $495

American stereoscopic viewer amusement machine in stained oak case, circa 1915, 42in. high. $540

AMERICANA

AMUSEMENT MACHINES

American totalisator one-armed bandit decorated with War Eagle, circa 1931, 27in. high. $660

American coin-operated mutoscope 'Death Dive', circa 1915, 50in. high. $680

Mutoscope by the International Mutoscope Reel Co., circa 1905, 74in. high. $710

Great Race game, coin-operated, in oak casing with glazed upper section, 47in. wide, circa 1925. $850

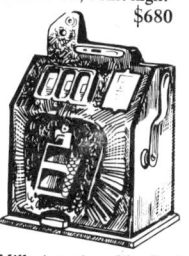

Mills American War Eagle slot machine finished in black on stained wooden base, 25½in. high, circa 1932. $870

Amusement machine by the International Mutoscope Reel Co. Ltd., America, circa 1915. $995

'Marco the Mystic' amusement machine in painted metal and wood cabinet, circa 1935, 69½in. high. $1,140

Automaton gum machine in upright oak case, 11½in. wide. $1,200

Mill's Perfect Muscle-Developing Owl Lifter amusement machine with cast iron base, circa 1904, 67½in. high. $1,760

AMERICANA

BOXES

Toleware circular spice cabinet, circa 1835, 6¼in. diam. $65

18th century black painted candle box, 11in. wide. $80

Art Nouveau glove box, circa 1890, of finely grained red leather, 13½in. long. $85

Late 19th century pine specimen chest. $115

Farmhouse salt box, circa 1780, 10¾in. high. $115

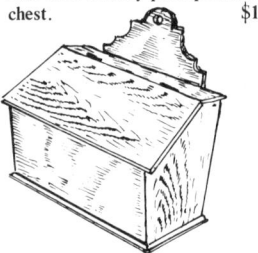

Oak candle box, circa 1790, 13in. wide. $160

Table square spice box with named sectioned interior, circa 1840. $170

Early 19th century covered oval quill work box with ivory finial, 5½in. long. $170

AMERICANA

BOXES

Miniature poplar decorated box, possibly Pennsylvania, circa 1800, 8½in. wide. $200

Early 19th century American decorated tin document box with domed cover, 13½in. long. $275

Mid 19th century American painted wooden folk art box with hinged cover, 12in. long. $275

Red tole painted tea caddy and writing box, circa 1790, 8in. wide. $300

An interesting American Civil War period Naval Paymaster's strongbox, 12 x 8 x 6in. $340

19th century homeopathic medicine chest with twenty four glass bottles, circa 1870, 9in. long. $420

18th century American candle box of octagonal form, 12¼in. long. $425

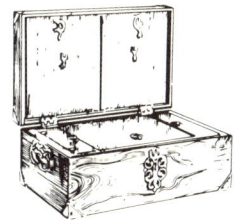

Antique mahogany brass-bound lift-top box, 15in. wide. $525

AMERICANA

BOXES

Early 19th century painted and decorated wall box, 11½in. wide. $615

Antique iron-bound oak decanter set, fully fitted, 16¾in. wide. $675

One of a pair of tin tea storage bins by Henry Troemner, Philadelphia, circa 1870, 22½in. high. $750

Early 19th century American carved and painted trinket box in pine, 10in. wide. $750

American pine candle box with carved decoration on all sides, 9¾in. long. $800

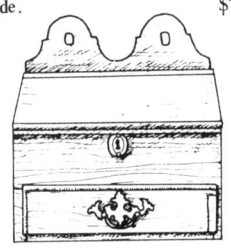

18th century American pine hanging wall candle box with double tombstone crest, 15in. wide. $800

Early 19th century tole decorated dome topped document box, 6¾in. high, New York. $825

18th century American decorated pine spoon rack, 12¾in. long. $850

AMERICANA

BOXES

Good Hepplewhite inlaid mahogany cellaret, 17¼in. wide, circa 1800. $900

A Micmac quilled birchbark box, 7½ x 6 x 5¼in. $900

Motorist's picnic service, circa 1920, fully fitted. $1,000

Good painted and decorated pine document box, 18in. long, circa 1800. $1,125

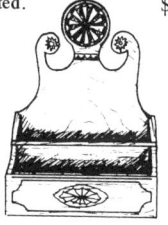

Early 19th century Federal mahogany wall box with scrolled crest, 7¼in. wide. $1,200

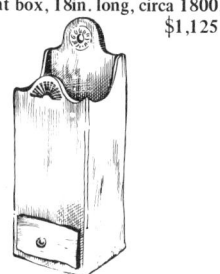

18th century New England cherrywood pipe box with scalloped front showing carved fan, 20½in. high. $1,350

18th century American mahogany pipe box with wall attachment, 16½in. high. $1,400

Painted poplar box, possibly Pennsylvania, circa 1800, with domed top, 7¼in. wide. $1,700

AMERICANA

BRONZE

American bronze figure, signed Paul Herzel, circa 1910. $250

Pair of early 20th century Tiffany bronze and enamel bookends, 13cm. high. $250

American bronze inkwell in the form of a crab, circa 1900, 10½in. long. $325

Late 17th century bronze candlestick with tapered stem, 10in. $450

Tiffany four-branch bronze candelabrum, 12¼in. high. $550

20th century American relief bronze wall fountain, signed H. Burton, 29¾in. wide. $575

AMERICANA

BRONZE

Modern bronze bust of an Indian, 14in. high. $845

Pair of Tiffany Studios gilt bronze candlesticks, circa 1900, 24cm. high. $985

Pair of mid 18th century Chippendale bell metal andirons, 20in. high. $1,000

Pair of Tiffany Studios silvered bronze candleholders, circa 1900, 40cm. high. $1,355

19th century American or European bronze statue of a man and a stag, 29in. wide, unsigned. $1,400

Bronze of an Indian warrior entitled 'Appeal to the Great Spirit', signed C. E. Dallin, 1913, 20in. high. $1,465

AMERICANA

BRONZE

Bronze part desk set by Tiffany, twelve pieces in all. $1,500

Pair of bronze candlesticks, with Doric column stems on circular molded bases, 8¼in. $1,500

A Western United States bronze depicting the shoeing of an immigrant farmer's horse, by Carl Kauba. $1,575

A pair of Art Nouveau gilt bronze jardinieres, circa 1900, 16½in. high. $1,870

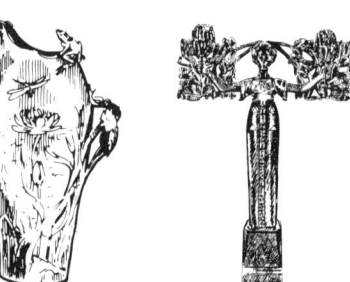

Bronze two-branched candelabrum, circa 1900, 19¼in. high. $1,965

AMERICANA

BRONZE

Bronze Indian fisherman, 26¾in. high. $2,250

Bronzed metal figure of a negro boy on a bamboo stool with a basket on his knee, 32in. high. $2,250

Fine bronze and iridescent Favrile glass six-branched candelabrum, by Tiffany, 15in. high. $4,500

Pair of Tiffany bronze and glass candlesticks, 14½in. high. $4,500

Fine bronze of a Red Indian, by Carl Kauba, on marble plinth, 19th century, 16in. high. $10,125

Late 18th century pair of colored bronze models of Red Indian chiefs, by C. Kauba. $13,500

AMERICANA

CARVED WOOD

Good Toleware polished chamberstick, circa 1840, 2½in. high, by H.F. & Co. $75

Sycamore wood butter marker, circa 1830, 5in. diam. $75

19th century American wooden handleless butter stamp with incised anchor, 3½in. diam. $75

Beechwood butter marker, circa 1840, 4½in. diam. $80

19th century American wooden butter stamp of shell design, 3½in. diam. $100

Carved wood and gilded eagle, circa 1810, 18½in. wide. $110

20th century wooden painted duck decoy with simulated green and white feathers. $120

American coconut shell carved with male and female portrait busts. $130

AMERICANA

CARVED WOOD

Early 19th century pinewood bowl, possibly American, 15in. diam. $145

18th century American carved gilded eagle, 7½in. high. $150

19th century American wooden butter stamp carved with a running fox, 2½in. diam. $150

19th century American wooden butter mold with double-sided pinwheel and tulip decoration, 4½in. diam. $150

19th century American wooden butter stamp carved with a cow, 3½in. diam. $150

20th century carved wooden decoy duck, 13½in. long. $200

20th century American woodcock carving on weatherbeaten log, 20cm. long. $200

19th century European wooden butter mold with eagle decoration, 6¼in. diam. $210

AMERICANA

CARVED WOOD

19th century American wooden butter stamp showing a bird on a branch, 3in. diam. $225

Early 20th century American painted and carved wood seagull, mounted on a board, 16½in. high. $225

18th century burl wood scoop of cup shape with cone handle, 5in. diam. $250

19th century American butter stamp, carved with a lamb, 3in. diam. $275

19th century American wooden butter stamp with incised deer, 4in. diam. $300

19th century carved wooden elephant with stand and trappings, 29in. long, possibly for P. J. Barnum. $300

AMERICANA

CARVED WOOD

19th century American wooden oval butter stamp with carved eagle standing on a globe, initials on either side, 5½in. long. $350

20th century American wooden horse's head mounted on a wall plaque, 20in. high. $350

Late 19th century rococo revival carved walnut wall shelf, 10½in. long. $350

A finely carved oak eagle from the 18th century, 21in. high, 23in. wide. $440

18th century round burl bowl, American, with rectangular handles, 11½in. diam. $450

Two American 19th century wooden flagons, 10in. and 9½in. high. $450

AMERICANA

CARVED WOOD

Late 16th century lesser yellow-leg in original paint, 10½in. high. $475

18th century New England handled wooden bowl, 15in. wide. $825

Late 18th century blackamoor tobacco counter figure, damaged, 23in. high. $800

One of a pair of 19th century carved carousel horses with brass harnesses and saddles, 46in. long. $850

American carved and polychrome painted wood panel, circa 1850, 9ft. long. $900

AMERICANA

CARVED WOOD

Pair of 19th century American carved Folk Art wooden deer, 42in. wide. $1,000

19th century American zebra carousel figure with saddle and harness, 58in. long. $1,150

Late 19th century American carved wood tobacconist's sign, 62in. high. $1,320

Stern board carving, circa 1900, 59in. wide. $1,900

Mid 19th century carved and painted rowboat with three figures, American, 13½in. long. $2,600

AMERICANA

CHANDELIERS

Early 19th century iron chandelier with scalloped edge, 19in. diam.
$350

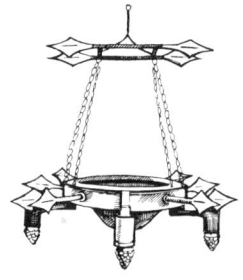

Early 19th century tin Argand-type chandelier, 35in. high. $400

Favrile glass and bronze chandelier, by Tiffany Studios, 20in. high. $1,260

Tiffany Studios leaded glass inverted basket-form shade, 525cm. diam.
$2,500

18th/early 19th century wood and iron painted chandelier, 38in. wide.
$2,600

Iridescent Favrile glass chandelier, by Tiffany, shade 14in. high. $3,035

AMERICANA

CHANDELIERS

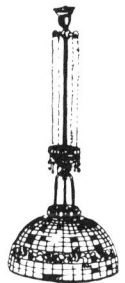

Unusual leaded glass chandelier with pulley pull-down mechanism, 52½in. high. $3,575

Gilt bronze and Favrile glass ceiling fixture, by Tiffany, 17in. high. $3,715

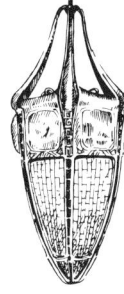

Favrile glass turtle-back and leaded glass chandelier, by Tiffany, 34½in. high. $14,625

Rare green glass and bronze chandelier by Tiffany, 46in. high. $15,000

Yellow rose bush leaded glass hanging lamp, by Tiffany, 24¾in. diam. $23,625

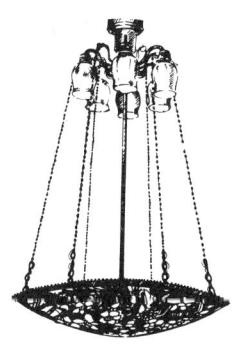

A rare calamander leaded glass chandelier, by Tiffany, 48in. high. $37,125

AMERICANA

CHINA

19th century black glazed pottery water jug. $20

Walley pottery basket-shaped vase, Massachusetts, circa 1910, 8¼in. diam. $100

19th century Lithophane lamp shade on brass frame, 7¼in. $100

One of a pair of acanthus leaf and scroll terracotta shelf brackets, 12½in. high, circa 1840. $110

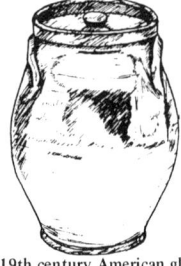

19th century American glazed redware pottery jar with cover, 10in. high. $130

One of two brown glazed pottery flasks, larger 25cm. high. $150

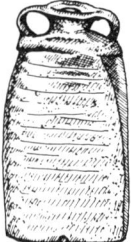

Stoneware square two-handled vase, 9½in. high. $150

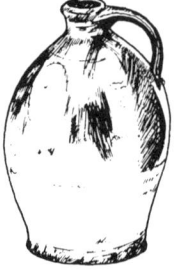

19th century American glazed redware pottery jug with handle, 9in. high. $160

Wheatley pottery vase, Cincinnati, Ohio, circa 1880, 9in. high. $175

AMERICANA

CHINA

Stoneware spirit flask molded on each side to show Rice, an American entertainer, 8in. high. $180

Newcomb pottery vase, New Orleans, circa 1910, signed A.S.F., 6in. high. $200

Glazed earthenware musical jug, circa 1935, 10in. high. $205

Rookwood pottery floral arrangement, 1921, 11in. high. $225

Paul Revere pottery vase, Brighton, Massachusetts, circa 1930. $225

Early 19th century American slipware decorated plate with crimped rim, 9¾in. diam. $225

Rare late 18th century American commemorative earthenware dish, 14¾in. diam. $235

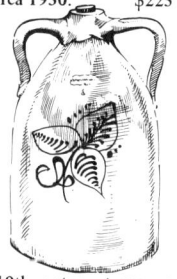

19th century stoneware double-handled jug, New York, 21in. high, with blue floral decoration. $250

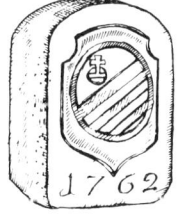

Stone lamp with wire and iron hinged door, dated 1762, 13in. high. $250

AMERICANA

CHINA

A Van Briggle Pottery Co. oviform vase of shaped outline, 26.5cm. high. $260

Grueby Art pottery vase, Boston, Massachusetts, circa 1910, 5¾in. high. $325

19th century American stoneware batter pitcher, 10in. high. $350

19th century stoneware decorated crock by Fulper Bros., Flemington, N.J., 10in. high. $350

Rookwood pottery standard glaze cornucopia vase with swirl rim, Cincinnati, Ohio, 1892, 6in. high. $400

Rookwood pottery iris glaze jar, Ohio, circa 1914, probably by Sara Alice Toohey, 7in. high. $400

Weller Sicardo vase, Fultonham, Ohio, circa 1905, 10½in. high. $400

Early 19th century American slipware decorated plate with crimped rim, 10¼in. diam. $425

Rookwood pottery ewer in sage green clay, Ohio, 1900, 8½in. high. $425

AMERICANA

CHINA

Early 19th century Redware pottery pitcher with high flared rim, 8¼in. high. $425

Rookwood pottery iris glaze vase, Ohio, circa 1908, 10½in. high, cracked. $475

Mid 19th century American stoneware decorated water cooler with domed cover, Pennsylvania, 21½in. high. $500

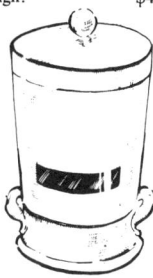

White apothecary pottery jar with gold lettering 'Leeches', 10in. high. $500

Rookwood pottery figure of a recumbent centaur, modeled by Wm. F. McDonald, 1931, 14in. long. $500

Rookwood pottery standard glaze mug, signed for Kataro Shirayamadani, circa 1887. $550

Mid 19th century chalkware sitting cat, Pennsylvania, 13½in. high. $550

19th century American Rogers group 'Why Don't You Speak For Yourself John?' $550

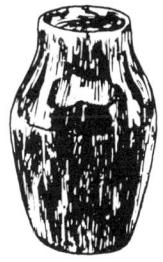

Dedham pottery experimental vase, Massachusetts, circa 1895, 7½in. high. $600

AMERICANA

CHINA

Early 19th century American stoneware jug with molded lip, 9in. high. $675

Mid 19th century chalkware sitting dog, Pennsylvania, 13¾in. high. $800

Mid 19th century chalkware rooster, Pennsylvania, 11in. high. $850

Rookwood pottery and Gorham silver mounted perfume bottle, Ohio, circa 1894, 3½in. high. $850

Newcomb pottery cylindrical vase, Louisiana, circa 1897, 7½in. high. $875

Rookwood pottery ewer, Cincinnati, 1889, with elongated neck, 14½in. high. $900

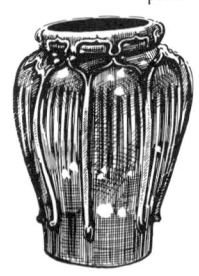

Grueby pottery lamp base, Boston, Massachusetts, circa 1910, 12in. high. $950

Rookwood standard glaze vase, signed A. R. Valentien, circa 1897, 11½in. high. $1,050

Rookwood bisque Spanish water jug, Ohio, circa 1883, 9½in. high. $1,250

AMERICANA

CHINA

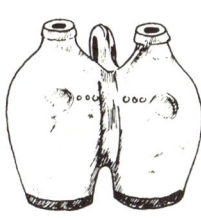

American double stoneware jug, 1830, with single handle. $1,250

Rookwood scenic vellum glaze vase, Ohio, circa 1919, 14½in. high. $1,300

Rookwood sterling overlay standard glaze jardiniere, Ohio, circa 1907, 5½in. high. $1,500

Rookwood pottery vellum glaze plaque, Ohio, circa 1919, 8¾in. high. $1,600

A Rookwood oviform vase mounted in silver as a ewer, 21cm. high. $2,000

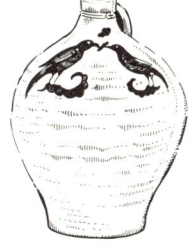

Early 19th century four gallon ovoid stoneware jug, Connecticut, 17¼in. high. $2,100

Newcomb pottery vase in blue, artist Leona Nicholson, circa 1903, 10½in. high. $2,100

Rookwood pottery matt glaze vase decorated with fish, 12¾in. high, Cincinnati, Ohio, circa 1901. $4,000

Rookwood pottery vellum vase, signed A. R. Valentien, 1905, 12in. high. $5,100

AMERICANA

CLOCK SETS

An Art Deco soft metal clock set, complete with side urns. $270

Bronze figure on onyx clock set, 21½in. long, circa 1920. $450

Art Deco clock set of unusual design. $1,180

Ormolu and marble clock garniture, circa 1900, dial signed Camerden and Foster, New York. $1,400

AMERICANA

CLOCK SETS

Enamel and gilt bronze clock set, by Tiffany. $1,485

An ormolu and white marble clock garniture the dial signed Tiffany & Co., New York, France. $2,600

Three-piece Tiffany & Co. champleve enamel clock garniture, the vase flanked by two seated putti. $3,600

Three-piece Renaissance style bronze and Dore bronze clock garniture by J.E. Caldwell, clock 74cm. high. $5,500

AMERICANA

LONGCASE CLOCKS

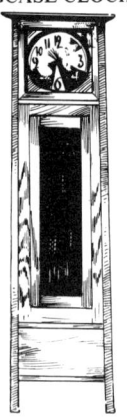

Mission oak tall clock by Waterbury Clock Co., circa 1910, 73in. high. $600

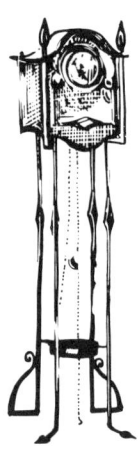

Wrought iron longcase clock, circa 1920, 65½in. high. $745

Chippendale style mahogany Westminster chimes longcase clock by D. Pratt's Son, Mass., 97in. high. $1,100

American Chippendale style mahogany tall cased musical clock, circa 1880, 98in. high. $1,300

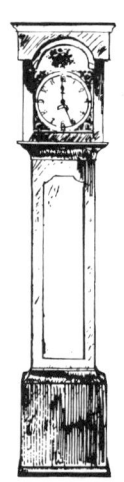

American cherrywood longcase clock 84in. high. $1,350

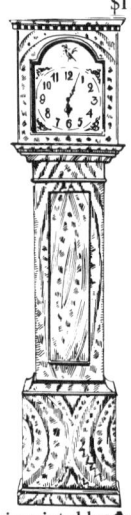

Grain painted longcase clock, New England, circa 1800, 86½in. high. $1,400

AMERICANA

LONGCASE CLOCKS

Chippendale style mahogany hall clock by Walter H. Durfee, circa 1898, 94½in. high. $2,050

Chippendale cherrywood longcase clock with broken arch, 95in. high. $2,100

19th century oak cased grandfather clock with brass face. $3,000

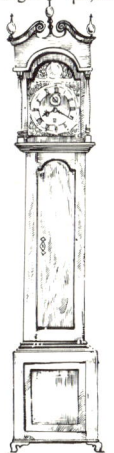

American Chippendale walnut longcase clock by Wm. Gillespie, Connecticut, late 18th century, 91in. high. $3,100

Federal mahogany inlaid longcase clock, dial inscribed S. Willard, Roxbury, circa 1790, 87in. high. $4,000

Federal cherry and mahogany veneer longcase clock, circa 1790, 86in. high. $5,500

AMERICANA

MANTEL CLOCKS

19th century American mantel clock in rosewood case. $55

Eight day American mantel clock, circa 1880. $100

American alarm clock by Jerome, circa 1880. $100

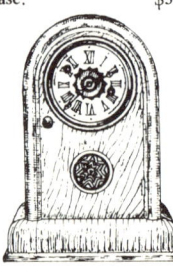

19th century walnut cased mantel clock with an American movement. $100

Heavy black marble and brass mounted clock by 'Ansonia Clock Co.', U.S.A. $100

Art Nouveau inlaid mahogany striking American clock, circa 1900, 15in. high. $150

American alarm clock, circa 1890. $160

Rococo revival walnut mantel clock, Ansonia, Connecticut, circa 1875, 23½in. high. $175

Late 19th century American mantel clock with alarm, in mahogany case, 12in. high. $180

AMERICANA

MANTEL CLOCKS

Late 19th century American cold painted cast iron 'Black Boy' timepiece, 1ft. 3½in. high. $270

Late 19th century glass and brass mantel clock sold by Shreve, Crump & Low, Boston, 12in. high. $325

Gilt metal carriage clock by Shreve Crump & Low, Boston, 6in. high. $650

Late 19th century American 'John Bull' cast iron clock by Bradley & Hubbard, 42cm. high. $725

American cast iron automaton clock in the form of a Negress, circa 1870, 16¼in. high. $835

Seth Thomas glass and brass mantel clock with enamel floral motif. $1,150

Ithaca parlor model calendar clock in walnut case, with double dial. $2,000

A porcelain mounted carriage timepiece, the dial signed Shreve, Crump & Low, Boston, 3¼in. high. $2,100

Shelf clock by Aaron Willard in inlaid mahogany case, circa 1820. $10,000

AMERICANA

WALL CLOCKS

19th century American rosewood framed wall clock. $125

Late 19th century American 'Ansonia' wall clock with mahogany case. $125

19th century American mahogany framed Seth Thomas wall clock. $140

American wall clock by Jerome & Co., New Haven, Connecticut. $150

Late 19th century American regulator wall clock in a mahogany case. $170

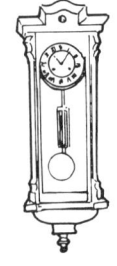

American wall clock with white enamel dial, in walnut case, 74cm. high. $225

E. Ingraham & Co., mahogany Ionic wall clock with reverse painted lower door, 21½in. high, circa 1880. $250

A fine 19th century American clock in a rosewood veneered case. $250

Inlaid American eight day clock, circa 1890, 2ft.4in. high. $225

AMERICANA

WALL CLOCKS

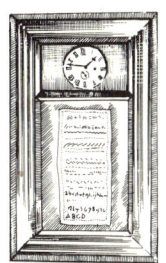

Empire rosewood veneered mirror clock, Connecticut, circa 1830, 36in. high. $425

An American walnut wall clock with glazed door and demi pillars to sides. $450

Pressed wood advertising figure-eight wall clock by Edward P. Baird & Co., New York circa 1880, 31in. long. $450

Late 19th century Gilbert calendar wall regulator timepiece, 45in. high, Winstead, Connecticut. $475

American Victorian walnut clock, circa 1875, 29½in. high. $500

Weight-driven rosewood veneer double dial calendar wall clock, Connecticut, circa 1865, 32in. high. $800

L. F. & W. W. Carter weight driven double dial calendar clock, 32in. high, late 19th century, Bristol, Connecticut. $875

Custom mahogany weight driven banjo timpeiece, dial signed Elmer O. Stennes, Mass. $950

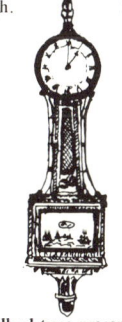

Willard type presentation banjo clock with acorn finial, 41in. high. $950

AMERICANA

WALL CLOCKS

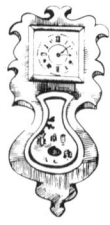

American mahogany wall acorn timepiece with painted tin dial, 28in. high. $1,200

Custom mahogany weight driven banjo timepiece with eagle finial. $1,200

Regulator wall timepiece by D. Pratt & Sons, Boston, 34in. high, circa 1850. $1,250

Early 20th century Waltham mahogany banjo clock, 40in. high. $1,250

Oak regulator wall timepiece inscribed, E. Howard & Co., Boston, 31½in. high. $1,400

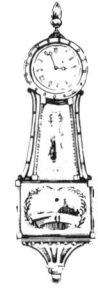

American Federal mahogany banjo clock, 46½in. high. $2,000

Mahogany banjo regulator with 8 day weight driven movement by Joshua Seward, Boston, 1831, 64in. high. $3,250

E. Howard gallery clock in walnut and burr veneered frame, 52½in. high, Boston, Massachusetts. $3,250

Walnut wall regulator by E. Howard & Co., 56in. high. $4,500

AMERICANA

WATCHES

Silver cased keyless free sprung reversed escape wheel lever pocket watch, unsigned, 44mm. diam. $300

Lady's gold fob watch, circa 1930. $300

Gold open faced keyless lever watch, hallmarked 1909, 53mm. diam. $495

American gold open face watch by E. Howard & Co., Boston, 53mm. diam. $500

Gold and enamel half-hunting cased keyless lever watch, 45mm. diam. $615

Rare American silver open faced chronometer watch by Hamilton Watch Co., 68mm. diam. $1,200

Gold open faced split seconds keyless chronograph by Tiffany & Co. $2,000

14kt. gold five-minute repeating pocket watch by The American Watch Co., Waltham. $2,880

An Elvis Presley wristwatch, by M. Tissot, 'Elvis Presley' in raised letters, circa 1970. $3,785

AMERICANA

COPPER & BRASS

American Art Deco copper water jug with spherical body, circa 1930, 12in. high. $45

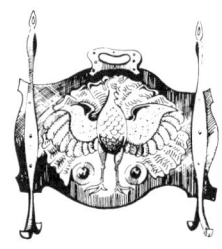

Art Deco brass sparkguard carved with a peacock. $90

Rare circular brass tripod candle reflector, circa 1880, 4½in. diam. $110

Large brass witch's hat phonograph horn, 31½in. high, circa 1908. $110

One of three American copper plaques, signed Raymond Averill Porter, circa 1913-19. $250

One of a pair of late 19th century cast brass bear candlesticks, 7¼in. high. $250

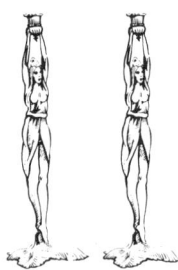

Pair of Art Nouveau figural candlesticks, in brass plated white metal, circa 1920, 18½in. high. $325

Late 17th century brass candlestick on tripod base, 7½in. high. $375

Pair of early 18th century brass candlesticks on saucer bases, 7¾in. high. $450

AMERICANA

COPPER & BRASS

American copper and gold leaf eagle, circa 1900, 20in. high. $450

One of a pair of early 19th century American Federal brass George Washington figural andirons. 21in. high. $500

Renaissance style brass andirons on curved legs, 82cm. high. $525

Early 19th century pair of brass andirons with shovel and tongs, American, 18in. wide. $600

Pair of late 18th century American brass andirons, 25in. high. $1,000

Pair of early 19th century Federal brass and wrought iron steeple-top andirons, 21in. high. $1,150

Early 19th century Regency brass bound pail with brass liner and handle, 35.5cm. high. $1,400

Pair of early 18th century brass candlesticks on saucer bases, 7½in. $1,550

One of a pair of late 17th century brass candlesticks, 8¾in. high. $4,100

AMERICANA

DOLLS

Early 20th century Shaker costumed bisque headed doll in gray wool dress, 15½in. high. $200

American 19th century painted wooden doll, 29cm. high. $215

China headed gentleman doll, 16in. high. $270

Composition portrait doll modeled as Shirley Temple. $350

American 'dancing dolls' automaton, circa 1880's, 10in. high, slightly damaged. $355

American Ives & Co. clockwork walking doll, circa 1880, 9½in. high. $560

Bisque head and shoulder dancing doll, 18in. high. $850

American Ives and Co. clockwork walking doll, 9½in. high, circa 1880. $900

Ragged cloth-made Izannah Walker doll. $2,150

AMERICANA

DOLLS' HOUSES

American diorama of an early 19th century hallway, circa 1950, fitted with dolls and furniture, 19½in. wide. $125

19th century wooden Mansard roof doll's house with painted brick front, 23¾in. high. $200

Early 20th century American wooden gabled roof doll's house with glass windows, 24¼in. high. $200

Late 19th/early 20th century wooden model of a stable with two papier-mache horses, 23in. wide. $250

Late 19th century American tin kitchen with stove, cupboard and pump, 19in. wide. $320

Painted wood doll's house with furniture and chattels. $1,580

AMERICANA

BEDS

19th century American Victorian walnut cradle on stand with shaped and pierced splats, 36in. high. $200

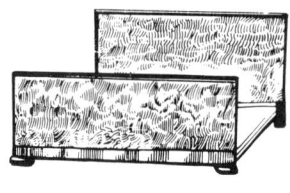

Bed from a three-piece set of Art Deco burl and ash bedroom suite, American, circa 1930. $250

Antique American tiger maple highpost bed, circa 1840, 60in. wide. $750

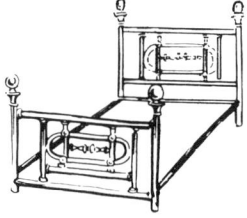

Late 19th century American Victorian brass bed of tube construction, 56in. wide. $900

Bed from a late 19th century American three-piece walnut bedroom set. $900

Late 19th century bed from a Renaissance revival walnut suite of five pieces. $1,050

AMERICANA

BEDS

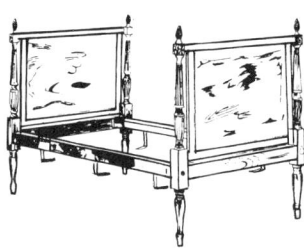

19th century American bed frame with paneled ends, 3ft.11½in. wide. $1,455

American Renaissance revival walnut and burl veneer bed with carved arch, sold with a matching commode, circa 1870. $1,500

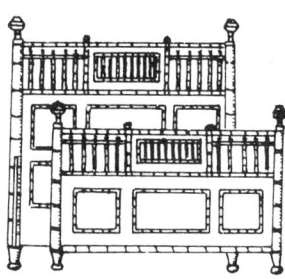

Victorian birch and bird's eye maple bed by R. J. Horner & Co., New York, circa 1870, 74in. long, sold with dressing table. $1,800

Bed from a late 19th century American Renaissance revival walnut bedroom suite, with burl panels. $1,900

American painted country bed in red and black, 50in. wide, circa 1800. $2,100

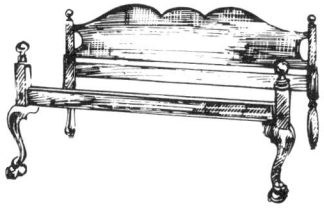

Rare Chippendale mahogany low-post bedstead, 52in. wide. $6,200

AMERICANA

BOOKCASES

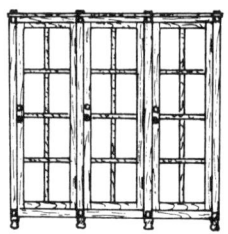

American Arts & Crafts oak bookcase, circa 1900, with three doors, 54in. wide. $200

Eastern United States Renaissance revival walnut bookcase, circa 1870, 46in. wide, with two glazed doors. $425

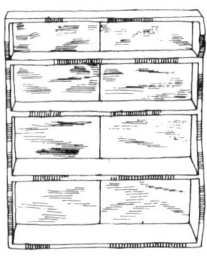

Early 19th century whale-end shelf, 37in. wide. $900

Hepplewhite style lady's desk with tapered legs, 31¼in. wide. $950

Gustav Stickley oak bookcase, New York, circa 1912, 39in. wide. $1,550

Gustav Stickley oak bookcase, New York, circa 1912, 53½in. wide. $1,600

AMERICANA

CABINETS

Arts & Crafts walnut carved and polychromed wall cabinet, 25¾in. wide. $400

Small Art Nouveau breakfront cabinet, circa 1900, 58in. wide. $730

Mid 19th century Victorian Renaissance revival buffet cabinet, American, 59in. wide. $750

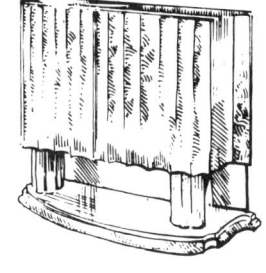

Stylish 1930's cocktail cabinet in pale walnut, 144cm. wide. $1,485

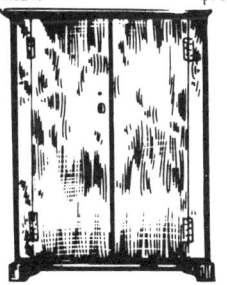

Late 18th century country maple canted wall cabinet, probably New Hampshire, 49½in. high. $2,100

One of a pair of American mahogany Egyptian revival cabinets, circa 1830, 24in. wide. $6,000

AMERICANA

CANDLESTANDS

William and Mary maple candlestand, New England, circa 1700, with octagonal top, 13in. wide. $275

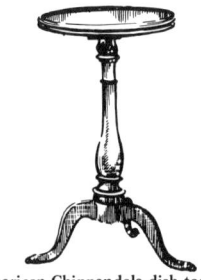

American Chippendale dish-top candlestand, circa 1780, 14½in. diam. $275

Early 18th century American pine and maple cross stretcher base candlestand, 27in. high. $425

American Federal mahogany inlaid tip-top candlestand, circa 1790, 28½in. high. $575

18th century elm candlestand with circular top and splayed pine legs, 17¼in. diam. $600

Early 19th century Shaker cherry and birch candlestand, Massachusetts, 26¾in. high. $700

AMERICANA

CANDLESTANDS

18th century American oak screw post lighting device, 47in. high. $700

Chippendale cherry tray top candlestand, American, 15 x 14½in. $900

American Federal mahogany candlestand, circa 1795, 23½in. high, with tilt-top. $1,300

Chippendale pine bird cage candlestand, New England, circa 1780, 14½in. diam. $1,795

Rare early 18th century turned maple lighting stand on three tapering legs, 43in. high. $2,400

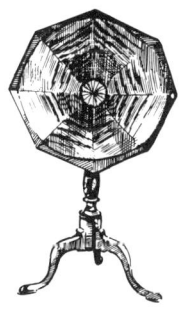

American Chippendale mahogany and mahogany veneer tilt-top candlestand, circa 1755, 23½in. wide. $7,000

AMERICANA

ARMCHAIRS

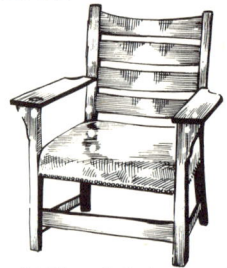

Gustav Stickley oak slat-back armchair, circa 1904, with original leather seat. $150

Late 19th century mahogany swivel chair with pierced splat. $160

American Arts & Crafts oak armchair with corniced rail, circa 1900, back 51in. high. $175

18th century armchair in fruitwood and beech with pierced crest, 45in. high. $225

Laminated mahogany armchair by the Paine Furniture Co., Boston, circa 1920, back 45in. high. $250

Mahogany armchair, 1890's, on turned legs. $250

AMERICANA

ARMCHAIRS

Stained beechwood armchair, circa 1890. $260

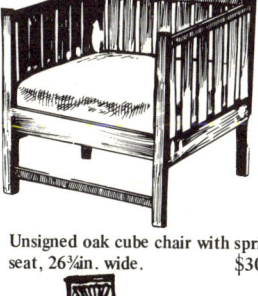

Unsigned oak cube chair with spring seat, 26¾in. wide. $300

One of a set of six oak dining chairs, circa 1900. $340

American Art Nouveau laminated mahogany and maple armchair, circa 1910, back 44½in. high. $350

One of a pair of American 20th century Gothic revival oak hall chairs, 72in. high. $400

One from a set of nine American William and Mary style armchairs, circa 1900, back of chair 49in. high. $475

AMERICANA

ARMCHAIRS

Large Art Deco giltwood tub chair, early 1920's. $495

Late 19th century Renaissance revival walnut Dante-style chair, American, 48in. high. $500

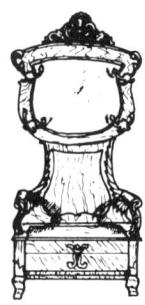

Late 19th century American Victorian oak hall tree, top with beveled glass mirror, 38½in. wide. $550

One of a pair of American chrome plated spring steel armchairs with fabric seats, circa 1930, back 42in. high. $550

Two rococo revival walnut chairs, America, circa 1860, with carved crests, 45in. and 40½in. high. $550

AMERICANA

ARMCHAIRS

One of a pair of Art Deco giltwood armchairs, early 1920's. $610

American William and Mary corner chair, 32in. high, circa 1700-30. $675

One of a pair of Art Deco tub chairs, early 1920's. $765

One of a pair of oak open armchairs, circa 1900, 31in. high. $845

A pair of 19th century Renaissance style armchairs. $850

AMERICANA

ARMCHAIRS

George II American open armchair in faded honey-color Virginia red walnut, circa 1745. $1,500

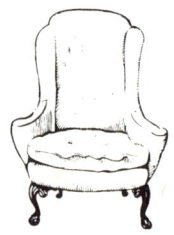

Late 18th century George III armchair with out-turned arms, back 46in. high. $1,650

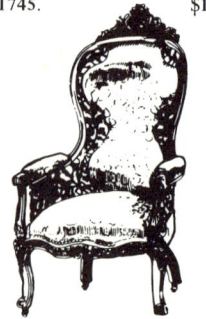

Victorian laminated rosewood armchair with carved crest and pierced back. $2,000

Chippendale mahogany corner chair, Boston, Massachusetts, circa 1755, restored. $2,100

Mid 19th century American Victorian laminated and carved rosewood armchair, 42½in. high. $2,100

Arts & Crafts lady's oak spindle Morris chair by Gustav Stickley, circa 1905. $2,300

AMERICANA

ARMCHAIRS

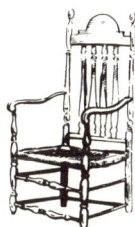

American William and Mary maple and ash banister armchair, circa 1700. $2,600

One of a pair of buffalo horn armchairs, by W. Friedrich, Texas. $4,275

Federal mahogany lolling chair with serpentine back, Massachusetts, circa 1780. $9,500

Mid 18th century Queen Anne walnut wing armchair with baluster turned stretcher base, 47in. high. $10,000

Gustav Stickley oak Morris chair with slanted arms, New York, circa 1906, 33in. wide. $10,000

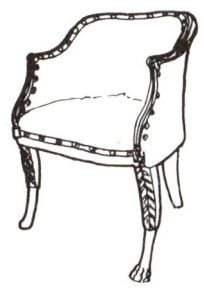

American library armchair attributed to Duncan Phyfe, circa 1815. $33,750

AMERICANA

LADDER BACK CHAIRS

American Queen Anne child's ladder back side chair with rush seat, circa 1765. $300

One of six Arts & Crafts oak side chairs, Gustav Stickley, New York, circa 1912. $300

One of a pair of four slat maple and ash side chairs, mid 18th century, New Hampshire, 43in. high. $550

18th century American ladder back armchair, 46in. high. $700

18th century child's maple ladder back high chair, 38½in. high. $2,500

One of a set of six mid 19th century New England ladder back dining chairs. $3,000

AMERICANA

ROCKING CHAIRS

A Victorian rocking chair with spindle spar back. $145

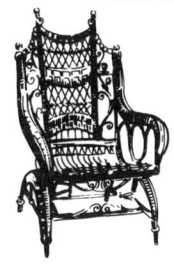

Late 19th century wicker platform rocker, American, height of back 46in. $175

American Elizabethan revival walnut platform rocker, New York, circa 1884. $275

American rocking chair with the original painted decoration, 42in. high, circa 1840. $360

American stained beechwood rocking chair with turned legs, circa 1880. $365

Gustav Stickley inlaid oak rocker, signed, 37in. high, seat missing. $2,400

AMERICANA

SIDE CHAIRS

 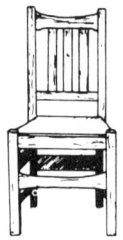

Two from a set of five Stickley Brothers oak chairs, circa 1915.
$100

Gustav Stickley oak side chair, New York, circa 1905, back 39in. high. $140

William and Mary banister back side chair, America, circa 1720, 43in. high. $140

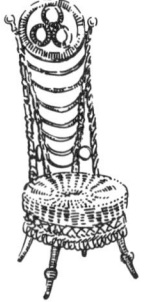

American wickerwork high back chair, circa 1880-1900. $370

19th century American rosewood nursing chair with curved and scrolled padded back. $390

AMERICANA

SIDE CHAIRS

Victorian laminated rosewood side chair with carved crest. $400

One of two matching transitional Queen Anne/Georgian side chairs. $550

William and Mary banister back side chair, New England, circa 1700. $625

One of a set of three thumb back side chairs, signed H. Cook, New England, circa 1820. $650

Two from a set of twelve Federal style mahogany chairs, 20th century, with pierced splats. $650

AMERICANA

SIDE CHAIRS

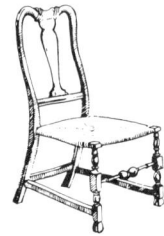

New England Queen Anne maple Spanish foot side chair with vase-shaped splat, circa 1730, back of chair 41½in. high. $700

One of a set of eight 19th century baroque style carved side chairs in oak, backs 53in. high. $800

American William and Mary banister back side chair, circa 1770, with carved crest. $850

One of a pair of late 19th century Eastern United States Victorian ebonized wood side chairs, 39in. high. $875

One of a set of six oak dining chairs, American, 20th century, with leather seats. $900

One of a pair of Queen Anne style side chairs, 41in. high, circa 1730-60. $900

AMERICANA

SIDE CHAIRS

One of a set of five early 19th century painted side chairs, 35½in. high. $1,000

One of a set of six American rush-seated stained elm and beech chairs, early 18th century. $1,180

One of a set of four rococo revival side chairs, American, circa 1865, with carved backs. $1,250

One of a pair of American Federal mahogany side chairs, circa 1810, 35½in. high. $1,300

Two from a set of six American 20th century Chippendale style mahogany chairs with pierced splats. $1,300

AMERICANA

SIDE CHAIRS

One of a set of eight Chippendale style mahogany chairs, American, 20th century. $1,400

One of a pair of 18th century Chippendale mahogany side chairs with pierced splats. $1,600

Chippendale mahogany side chair with serpentine crest rail, Massachusetts, circa 1770. $1,700

One of a set of six Chippendale style mahogany side chairs. $1,750

Two from a set of four 20th century American Queen Anne mahogany dining chairs, chair back 40in. high. $2,500

AMERICANA

SIDE CHAIRS

One of a set of six rococo revival side chairs, American, circa 1865, with carved backs. $2,500

One of a set of five Federal cherrywood side chairs, circa 1795, 37in. high. $2,600

One of a set of six Sheraton tiger maple fancy chairs, circa 1820, with balloon seats. $3,000

One of a set of six painted arrow back side chairs, Massachusetts, circa 1820. $3,000

William and Mary carved side chair, early 18th century, New England, 47½in. high. $4,000

One of a set of six George II mahogany dining chairs, possibly American. $11,250

AMERICANA

WINDSOR CHAIRS

One of a set of ten hardwood spindle-backed Windsor chairs. $495

Mid 18th century American fan back Windsor side chair, 36in. high. $600

Mid 18th century knuckle arm Windsor chair with bow back and bobbin turned stretchers. $825

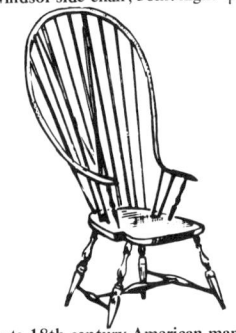

Late 18th century American maple, ash and pine brace back armchair, 44in. high. $1,150

One of a set of six 18th century fan back Windsor side chairs, New Hampshire, 35½in. high. $1,600

Late 18th century American writing-arm Windsor chair with saddle seat, 29in. high. $1,800

AMERICANA

WINDSOR CHAIRS

Late 18th century American brace back Windsor armchair, 38½in. high. $2,000

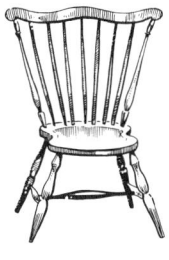

One of a set of four fan back Windsor side chairs, New England, circa 1800. $2,500

Mid 18th century bow back Windsor armchair, New England, 35¼in. high. $2,700

One of a set of seven step down Windsor side chairs, circa 1800, 35in. high. $3,000

One of a set of three late 18th century fan back Windsor chairs with shaped crest rails. $3,800

One of a set of six painted step down side chairs, American, circa 1800, 34½in. high. $4,400

AMERICANA

CHESTS

Late 17th century walnut storage chest with paneled front, 40in. long. $350

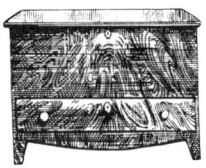

Country Federal grain painted blanket chest with lift top, 44¼in. wide, circa 1810. $350

American country pine grain bin with slant lid, circa 1810, 45in. wide. $475

Antique American Greek revival painted cellarette, Baltimore, circa 1800, with tapering sides. $550

American painted and decorated blanket box, dated 1732, restored, 36in. wide. $675

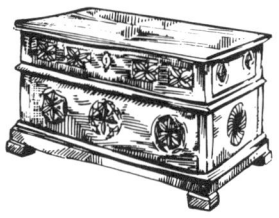

Early 18th century carved and stained pine chest, 4ft.6½in. wide. $800

Marquetry inlaid mahogany lift top chest, 61½in. long, with brass banding. $850

American painted blanket chest with lift top, 42½in. wide. $1,000

AMERICANA

CHESTS

18th century Canadian country birch and pine storage box with lift top, 43in. wide. $1,200

American painted basswood dower chest, circa 1780, 51in. wide, on bracket feet. $1,300

Late 18th century pine decorated dower chest, Pennsylvania, 48in. wide. $1,700

Plymouth pine blanket chest, circa 1700, 49½in. wide. $2,455

Decorated pine blanket box, New York, dated 1816, 39¾in. wide, with hinged molded top. $4,100

Rare carved pine child's blanket box, New England, 1788, 21¼in. wide. $4,300

Georgian chinoiserie black lacquer chest on stand, 42in. wide. $5,250

Early 18th century William and Mary oak and pine chest on frame, with lift top, 30in. wide. $6,500

AMERICANA

CHESTS OF DRAWERS

Art Deco burl maple chest of drawers, circa 1925, 51¾in. wide. $565

19th century provincial oak three-drawer commode with applied molding, 34in. wide. $625

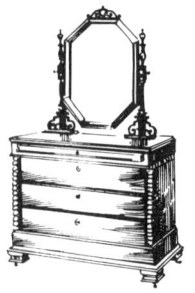

American rosewood chest of drawers with octagonal mirror, 37in. wide. $730

Early 19th century grain painted blanket chest, New England, with lift top case, 38¼in. wide. $850

American Chippendale pine tall blanket chest with lift top, circa 1780, 40¼in. wide. $900

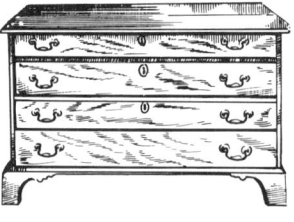

American Chippendale birch chest of drawers, circa 1800, 40in. wide handles replaced. $900

AMERICANA

CHESTS OF DRAWERS

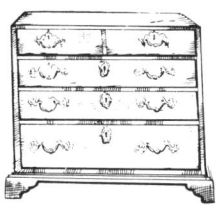

18th century George II walnut commode with brass handles and escutcheons, 38in. wide. $950

Late 17th century William and Mary walnut chest, on four ball feet. $950

American Victorian walnut chest of six drawers, circa 1860, 24½in. wide. $1,000

American Chippendale mahogany bow-front chest of four drawers, 44in. wide. $1,200

Federal grain painted blanket chest, Vermont, circa 1800, 39½in. wide, with two drawers. $1,200

American Federal maple inlaid chest with rectangular top and bow-front, circa 1790, 38½in. wide. $1,200

AMERICANA

CHESTS OF DRAWERS

Art Deco burl maple chest of drawers, 63¾in. high. $1,250

Federal mahogany and curly maple veneer bow-fronted chest of drawers, 41½in. wide, circa 1800. $1,300

American Chippendale curly maple tall chest of drawers, circa 1780, 39½in. wide. $1,400

American Chippendale pine two-drawer blanket chest, with simulated five-drawer front, circa 1765, 37in. wide. $1,500

Mid 18th century New England Chippendale pine chest of drawers, 33¾in. wide. $1,600

Country Chippendale tiger maple chest of drawers, 48in. high, circa 1770, on dove-tailed bracket feet. $1,800

AMERICANA

CHESTS OF DRAWERS

American Chippendale serpentine fronted chest of drawers, circa 1780, 43¾in. wide. $1,900

American Chippendale tall chest, New England, circa 1780, 39¼in. wide. $2,100

New England Chippendale tiger maple tall chest of drawers with applied molded cornice, 36in. wide, circa 1760. $2,200

Country Federal grain painted chest of drawers, 41in. wide, circa 1795. $2,300

American Chippendale maple and pine tall chest of drawers, circa 1780, 41in. wide. $2,500

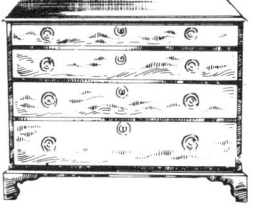

Chippendale cherrywood chest of drawers, New England, circa 1780, 42in. wide. $2,600

AMERICANA

CHESTS OF DRAWERS

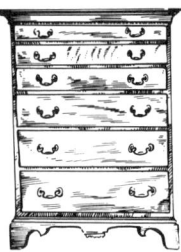

American Chippendale maple chest of drawers, circa 1780, 36¾in. wide. $2,700

American Chippendale cherrywood tall chest of drawers with molded cornice, 36in. wide. $2,750

American Chippendale tiger maple chest of drawers, 37½in. wide. $3,000

Late 18th century Connecticut Chippendale reverse-serpentine cherrywood chest of drawers, 42in. wide. $3,400

Mid 18th century American country Chippendale birch tall chest with applied cornice, 36in. wide. $3,400

Chippendale cherrywood tall blanket chest, New England, circa 1760, 36in. wide, with lift top. $3,500

AMERICANA

CHESTS OF DRAWERS

American Chippendale mahogany serpentine fronted chest of drawers, circa 1770, 38¾in. wide. $4,000

Late 18th century New England Chippendale tiger maple chest of drawers, 40in. wide, restored. $4,100

Chippendale walnut chest on stand, 42in. wide, circa 1760. $4,250

American Queen Anne pine lift top blanket chest with simulated drawer front, circa 1740, 38¾in. wide. $10,500

Country William and Mary pine and maple painted chest of drawers, Deerfield, Massachusetts, 1700-1715, 40in. wide. $14,000

18th century Massachusetts mahogany chest of drawers with brass handles and escutcheons. $21,000

AMERICANA

CHESTS ON CHESTS

Chippendale style mahogany chest on chest with broken arch top, on ogee bracket feet, 42in. wide. $1,200

American Chippendale maple chest on chest, 40in. wide, circa 1780. $2,500

Chippendale cherrywood chest on chest, Pennsylvania, circa 1770, 38in. wide. $2,500

Late 19th century American custom Chippendale mahogany and mahogany veneer block front chest on chest, 40in. wide. $3,100

Mid 18th century Chippendale tiger maple chest on chest, New Hampshire, 36in. wide. $4,500

18th century American Chippendale cherrywood bonnet top chest on chest, 53in. wide. $5,250

AMERICANA

CHINA CABINETS

Victorian Renaissance revival ebonized wood cabinet, 19in. wide, circa 1865. $350

Early 20th century American Victorian oak china cabinet with molded top, 46in. wide. $600

Mahogany cabinet, circa 1895, 68½in. high. $1,000

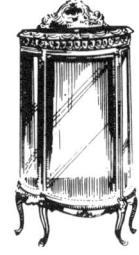

20th century American custom Renaissance revival giltwood curio cabinet, 27in. wide. $1,300

American mahogany and mahogany veneer bow-fronted china cabinet, circa 1895, 55¼in. wide. $1,500

Mahogany display cabinet with arched mirrored top, 38½in. wide, circa 1900. $1,850

AMERICANA

CUPBOARDS

Late 19th century American Renaissance revival carved walnut whatnot, over cupboard base, 40in. wide. $525

American Chippendale pine corner cupboard, circa 1780, 42½in. wide. $650

American rosewood commode with molded marble top, 43in. wide. $730

One of two matching walnut commodes, New England, circa 1870, one double and one single. $800

American pine corner cupboard with molded cornice, 41in. wide. $850

American country Federal grain painted pine cupboard, circa 1800, 49½in. wide. $900

AMERICANA

CUPBOARDS

18th century American pine step back cupboard, 38in. wide. $1,100

Mahogany buffet, circa 1895, 64in. high. $1,125

American pine corner cupboard with dentil frieze and bracket feet, 52in. wide. $1,150

18th century American country pine step back cupboard, 44in. wide. $1,200

American painted kas, New England, circa 1800, with molded cornice, 55in. wide. $1,200

Late 18th cenutry New England pine cupboard with open top, 32½in. wide. $1,300

AMERICANA

CUPBOARDS

One of a pair of American custom oak cupboards with galleried cornice top, circa 1920, 43½in. wide. $1,350

Late 18th century American Chippendale basswood corner cupboard, 45in. wide. $1,400

Late 18th century American pine cupboard with flat cornice, 48in. wide. $1,400

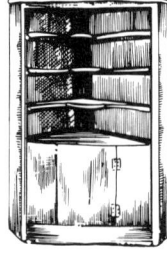

Early 19th century Federal painted pine corner cupboard, 50in. wide. $1,400

Mid 18th century American palladian pine built-in wall cupboard, 42in. wide. $1,700

Late 18th century American pine grain painted corner cupboard with molded cornice, 46in. wide. $2,000

AMERICANA

CUPBOARDS

American Federal cherrywood pie safe with double doors, circa 1795, 40in. wide. $2,000

Good painted and grained pine corner cupboard, circa 1750, 33in. wide. $2,250

18th century painted pine hanging cupboard, Pennsylvania, 23in. wide. $2,400

American country pine grain painted cupboard, circa 1800, 73in. high. $2,900

Late 18th century American country Chippendale corner cupboard with open shelves, 43in. wide. $3,600

18th century American country pine pewter dresser with molded cornice, 81in. wide. $4,500

AMERICANA

DESKS

Crafters oak drop-front desk, Cincinnati, circa 1910, 42in. wide. $200

Late 19th century American Victorian mahogany slant top desk with gallery top, 25in. wide. $375

American Victorian rosewood and walnut desk on frame, 22in. wide, circa 1870. $450

Rococo revival rosewood Davenport desk with pierced brass gallery, 22½in. wide. $500

Gustav Stickley oak fall front desk with pine compartments, New York, circa 1905, 31¾in. wide. $550

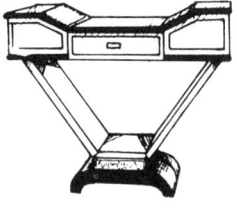

American Art Deco sycamore and mahogany desk with V-shaped top surrounded by walnut banding, 36¼in. wide, circa 1920. $600

AMERICANA

DESKS

Lady's Eastlake walnut and burl veneer desk with mirrored top, circa 1870, 31in. wide. $625

Late 19th century Louis XV style gilt and painted bureau de dame by R. J. Horner & Co., New York, 28in. wide. $800

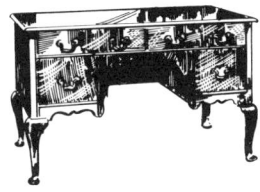

Queen Anne style walnut kneehole desk with crossbanded top, 51in. wide. $825

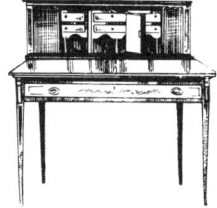

19th century American Hepplewhite mahogany tambour desk, 32¾in. wide. $900

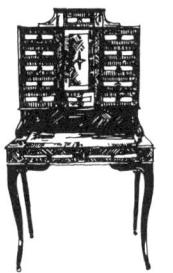

Secretary desk and stepped back drawer and cabinet arrangement, 18th century, 36in. wide. $1,000

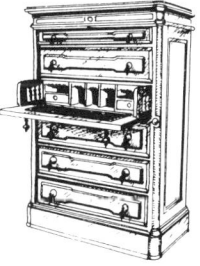

Late 19th century American Victorian walnut butler's desk, 40in. wide. $1,000

AMERICANA

DESKS

Queen Anne style oak desk on stand with slant top, 32in. wide. $1,400

Custom Hepplewhite mahogany tambour desk, 35½in. wide, with satinwood inlay. $1,400

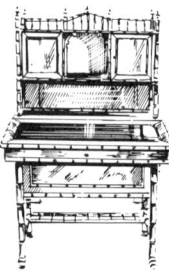

American Victorian bird's-eye maple veneer bamboo Davenport desk, circa 1870, 32in. wide. $1,800

American Chippendale mahogany slant top desk, circa 1770, 38½in. wide. $1,800

Chippendale maple and birch slant top desk, New England, circa 1780, 39¼in. wide. $1,900

Mid 19th century American Shaker pine bureau with tambour top, 39½in. wide. $2,100

AMERICANA

DESKS

American mahogany and oak bureau with sloping hinged lid, 40in. wide. $2,350

American Chippendale mahogany slant top bureau on bracket feet, circa 1780, 41¼in. wide. $2,400

American Federal mahogany inlaid bow-front secretaire chest, circa 1795, 42in. wide. $2,800

American Chippendale mahogany slant top desk, circa 1780, 36in. wide. $2,900

American Chippendale maple slant front desk, circa 1755, 37½in. wide. $3,000

An American port office desk with a finely fitted interior. $3,000

AMERICANA

DESKS

18th century American mahogany bureau, lid carved with a shell, 41in. wide. $3,290

Antique American mahogany ox-box desk, Massachusetts, circa 1760, 42in. wide. $3,500

Late 19th century American desk by the Wootton Desk Co., Indianapolis. $3,600

American Chippendale mahogany serpentine slant top desk, circa 1780, 51in. wide. $3,800

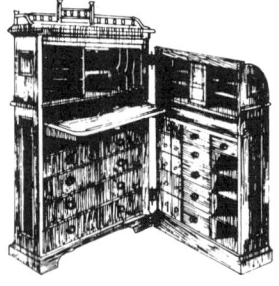

19th century North American oak office desk, 4ft.9in. wide, circa 1880. $4,000

Chippendale cherry and pine slant front desk, circa 1780, 37½in. wide. $4,250

AMERICANA

DESKS

Federal cherry inlaid slant top desk, circa 1790, 40½in. wide. $4,250

American mahogany ox-box slant top desk, Massachusetts, circa 1760, 41½in. wide. $4,600

Oak Wootton desk with maple-lined interior, 1874, 55in. wide. $4,740

18th century Massachusetts Chippendale reverse-serpentine mahogany bureau, 43½in. wide. $4,750

Late 19th century 'Wells Fargo' mahogany office cabinet. $5,000

American Chippendale maple slant top desk, 40in. wide. $5,000

AMERICANA

DESKS

Late 18th century Federal mahogany inlaid desk, Pennsylvania, 42in. wide. $5,000

18th century New England Chippendale reverse-serpentine birchwood bureau, 41in. wide. $5,500

Sheraton rosewood tambour front bureau, outlined with boxwood stringing, 36in. wide. $5,750

Mid 18th century American Chippendale tiger maple and maple slant top desk, 39in. wide. $6,000

19th century walnut Wootton Patent Office desk with galleried top, 58in. wide. $6,370

American 'Wells Fargo' desk by Wootton & Co., 42½in. wide. $6,750

AMERICANA

DESKS

American Queen Anne birch desk on frame with cut-out skirt, 35in. wide, circa 1750. $7,500

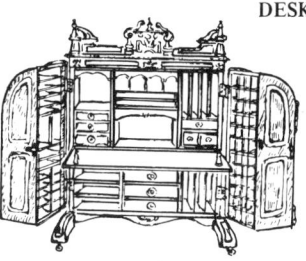

Late 19th century Wootton 'Wells Fargo' desk with satin walnut interior. $8,000

A good quality American Colonial bureau made in about 1765. $12,500

An 18th century Massachusetts mahogany kneehole desk. $22,500

Queen Anne tiger maple slant front desk, circa 1760, 36in. wide. $24,570

Mid 18th century American kneehole desk attributed to Edmund Townsend of Rhode Island, 92.7cm. wide. $200,000

AMERICANA

HIGHBOYS

American Chippendale style mahogany bonnet top highboy, circa 1930, 38½in. wide. $800

19th century American custom William and Mary walnut and burr veneer inlaid flat-top highboy, 39¾in. wide. $800

Custom Chippendale mahogany highboy with broken arch top, 36in. wide. $1,300

19th century walnut bow-fronted highboy with crossbanded borders, 3ft.2in. wide. $1,600

20th century American Chippendale style mahogany tallboy with broken arch top, 39in. wide. $1,650

American cherrywood Queen Anne highboy on cabriole legs, 36in. wide. $2,200

AMERICANA

HIGHBOYS

Queen Anne birch highboy, New England, circa 1760, with molded cornice, 37¼in. wide. $3,500

George I maple tallboy, on cabriole legs. $4,000

Queen Anne chest on stand, drawers framed by herringbone bands, 39in. wide. $4,015

Queen Anne tiger maple chest on stand, late 18th century, 38in. wide. $4,100

Queen Anne cherrywood and maple highboy, New England, circa 1770, 37in. wide. $4,250

American Queen Anne maple highboy, circa 1760, 38¼in. wide, with flat molded cornice. $5,250

AMERICANA

HIGHBOYS

American Queen Anne maple highboy, circa 1760, 36½in. wide. $5,500

Early 18th century American Queen Anne walnut bonnet top highboy, 39in. wide. $6,000

Late 18th century American Chippendale walnut chest on stand, 48¾in. wide. $6,000

American William and Mary maple and pine highboy, circa 1710, 40in. wide. $7,500

Queen Anne cherrywood highboy, American, circa 1730, 36in. wide. $8,000

American Chippendale maple highboy with molded cornice and dentil carving, 76in. high, circa 1760. $8,500

AMERICANA

HIGHBOYS

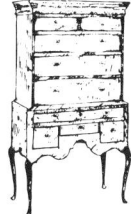

American Queen Anne mahogany highboy, New England, circa 1740, on cabriole legs, 34½in. wide. $9,000

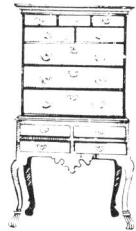

18th century New Jersey Queen Anne stained wood chest on stand on cabriole legs, 42in. wide. $10,000

Queen Anne curly maple highboy, 38in. wide. $12,000

Queen Anne maple highboy, 38½in. wide, circa 1730-60. $12,000

Queen Anne walnut, mahogany and cherrywood highboy, circa 1770, 38¾in. wide. $15,000

Late 18th century Queen Anne maple chest on chest, 38in. wide, with original brasses. $18,000

AMERICANA

LOWBOYS

Queen Anne mahogany lowboy with shell-carved drawer, 31in. wide. $600

William and Mary lowboy in mahogany and mahogany veneer, 30½in. wide. $850

Queen Anne style chinoiserie lacquered lowboy, 36in. wide. $850

Queen Anne walnut dressing table with inlaid top and cabriole legs, 38in. wide. $950

American Chippendale walnut lowboy with shell carvings, 39in. wide. $1,600

Early 18th century William and Mary walnut and maple dressing table 26in. wide. $2,500

AMERICANA

LOWBOYS

American Queen Anne cherrywood lowboy, circa 1760, 32½in. wide, restored. $2,750

American Queen Anne maple lowboy, circa 1760, with central carved fan, 28¾in. wide. $7,250

Queen Anne porringer top lowboy, circa 1750, with fan carved drawer, 38in. wide. $12,000

Queen Anne cherrywood dressing table with central fan carved drawer, 30in. wide, circa 1760. $14,000

Queen Anne cherrywood lowboy, circa 1750, 33in. wide. $17,000

Queen Anne walnut lowboy, 35½in. wide, circa 1750. $13,200

AMERICANA

SECRETAIRE BOOKCASES

American Empire mahogany secretary desk with glazed doors, 42in. wide. $600

American Chippendale style mahogany secretaire bookcase, circa 1920, 37in. wide. $1,100

20th century Custom mahogany and mahogany veneer Federal style secretary, Brookline, Massachusetts, 38in. wide. $1,150

American mahogany secretaire bookcase with Gothic glazed doors, 38in. wide. $1,400

Federal mahogany secretaire desk, New England, circa 1810, 41in. wide. $2,000

Early 19th century American mahogany writing cabinet, 4ft.2in. wide. $2,250

AMERICANA

SECRETAIRE BOOKCASES

American figure mahogany and satinwood lined cylinder secretaire bookcase, 4ft.1in. wide. $2,925

American Renaissance revival walnut and burl veneer roll-top secretaire, circa 1865, 53in. wide. $3,000

18th century Georgian mahogany secretaire cabinet, 42in. wide. $3,750

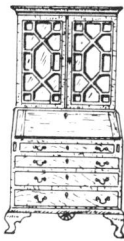

American Chippendale veneer secretary bookcase, circa 1770, 41in. wide. $5,500

Late 18th century Chippendale cherrywood serpentine secretaire bookcase, Central Massachusetts, 39¾in. wide. $19,000

18th century New England tiger maple secretaire bookcase with bonnet top, 38½in. wide. $20,000

AMERICANA

SETTEES & SOFAS

Late 19th century American Renaissance revival finger carved walnut sofa, 68in. long. $300

American Renaissance revival walnut and burl walnut settee, circa 1870, 61in. wide. $325

Late 19th century American walnut sofa with floral and acanthus carved framework, 7ft. wide. $500

19th century American mahogany settee on hairy claw feet, 83½in. wide. $520

Gustav Stickley V-back oak settee with leather seat, 47in. wide. $600

Mid 19th century American rococo revival walnut sofa with carved arm supports and apron. $600

AMERICANA

SETTEES & SOFAS

20th century American custom mahogany Chippendale settee with straight open back, 60in. wide. $625

Mid 19th century American mahogany sofa with curved triple arched back, 61in. wide. $830

Jacobean carved oak settle, with animal-form hand rests, 76in. long. $850

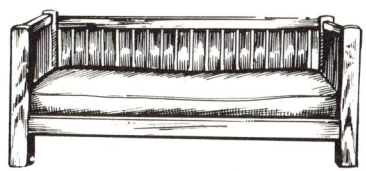

Unsigned oak settle, circa 1910, 76in. wide, with spring cushion. $850

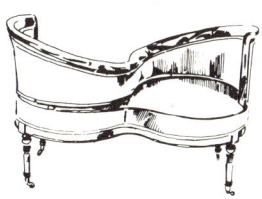

19th century Regency mahogany tete-a-tete with S-form back, 46in. long. $850

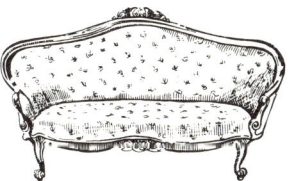

Eastern United States rococo revival walnut sofa, circa 1865, 78in. long. $1,000

AMERICANA

SETTEES & SOFAS

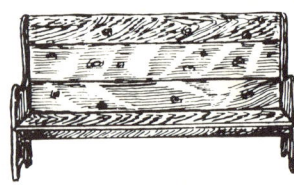

18th century American country pine settle with shaped sides, 75in. long. $1,150

One of a pair of late 19th century American rococo revival rosewood reclaimers, 51in. long. $1,150

18th century country beech settle with paneled and curved back, 72in. long. $1,400

Mahogany Chippendale style settee with camel back, on six curved legs, 77in. wide. $1,500

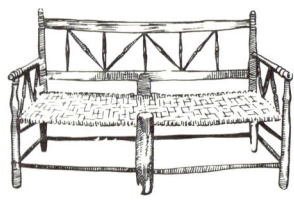

18th century New England wagon seat with turned spindle back, 34in. wide. $1,650

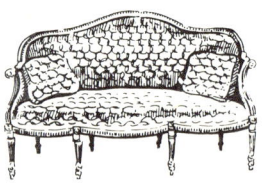

Late 18th century George III gray-painted sofa, 72in. wide. $1,855

AMERICANA

SETTEES & SOFAS

Mahogany Chippendale three-backed settee with vase-shaped splats, 69in. wide. $1,900

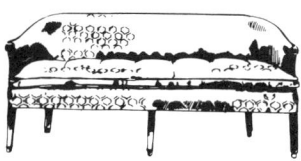

Hepplewhite mahogany sofa with molded scrolling arm rests, 79in. long. $1,900

Federal mahogany sofa, Pennsylvania, circa 1810, with rolled crest, 75in. long. $2,100

19th century George III style 'satyr and mask' settee, in mahogany, 51in. long. $3,600

One of a pair of mid 19th century carved rosewood meridiennes by John Henry Belter. $19,000

Superb mid 19th century American settee by John H. Belter of New York, in laminated rosewood frame. $38,430

AMERICANA

SIDEBOARDS

Victorian oak sideboard, American, with mirror back, circa 1900, 48in. wide. $250

Custom mahogany Jacobean style sideboard with carved gallery, 58in. wide. $375

American oak sideboard, top with two leaded glass doors, circa 1900, 43in. wide. $400

Federal mahogany and mahogany veneer sideboard, circa 1810, with shaped crest, 54½in. wide. $600

American rococo revival walnut and burled veneered sideboard, circa 1870, 49in. wide. $600

Eastlake cherry sideboard with carved bee and brickwork, circa 1875, 45in. wide. $650

AMERICANA

SIDEBOARDS

American mahogany sideboard with bowed three-quarter galleried top, 66½in. wide. $680

Late 19th century American Renaissance revival ebonized inlaid sideboard, 67in. wide. $700

Early 19th century George III sideboard in mahogany and mahogany veneer, 71½in. wide. $780

American Louis XV influence rosewood and rosewood veneer sideboard, circa 1930, 50in. wide. $800

American Victorian walnut sideboard with carved and molded top crest, circa 1870, 50in. wide. $900

Gustav Stickley oak sideboard with plate rack, signed, 56in. wide. $900

AMERICANA

SIDEBOARDS

American Federal style mahogany inlaid sideboard with bowed front, circa 1920, 45½in. wide. $950

American baroque style oak sideboard with carved crest, circa 1900, 64½in. wide. $1,150

Late 18th century George III mahogany sideboard, 7ft. wide. $1,500

Late 18th/early 19th century George III bow-front mahogany sideboard, 72in. wide. $1,500

Late 18th century George III demi-lune sideboard in mahogany, 71in. long. $1,650

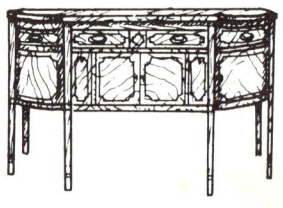

American Federal mahogany and mahogany veneer sideboard, circa 1790, 68¾in. wide. $1,800

AMERICANA

SIDEBOARDS

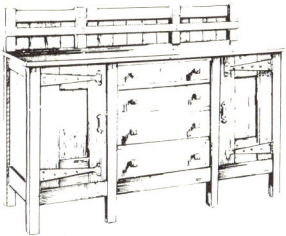

Gustav Stickley oak sideboard with rectangular top and ledge back, 178cm. wide. $1,820

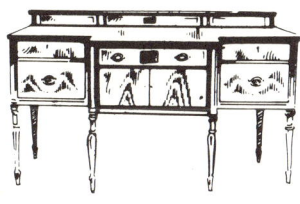

Federal mahogany inlaid sideboard, Middle Atlantic States, circa 1800, 67in. wide. $2,500

Federal mahogany and mahogany veneer sideboard, circa 1790, 72½in. wide. $2,500

Late 18th century George III serpentine front sideboard in mahogany, 72in. long. $2,600

Federal mahogany and mahogany veneer sideboard, circa 1790, 67in. wide. $2,600

American Sheraton mahogany bow-front serving board, circa 1810, 45in. wide. $7,250

AMERICANA

STANDS

American Federal mahogany bidet stand with kidney-shaped cutout, 19in. high. $100

Victorian carved rosewood canterbury, American, circa 1860, 23½in. wide. $325

American Sheraton inlaid mahogany night table, circa 1800, with square top, 32½in. high. $325

Early 19th century Empire style planter with copper insert, 44in. wide. $350

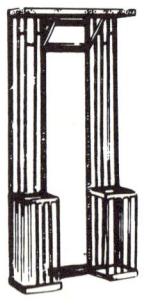

Art Deco wrought iron hall stand, circa 1920. $365

18th century American painted pine water bench, upper shelf with splashback, 26½in. wide. $400

AMERICANA

STANDS

Late 19th century American Renaissance revival marble top stand, 16in. wide. $425

American country painted book stand, circa 1800, with slanted top, 8¾in. high. $470

American country string quartet music stand, 50in. high, circa 1800. $500

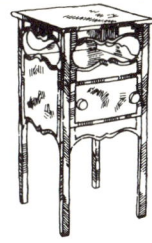

Early 19th century American Federal grain painted stand, 15in. wide. $550

Hepplewhite corner washstand, late 18th century. $600

Late 19th century American walnut pedestal with caryatid supports. $650

AMERICANA

STANDS

Mid 19th century American Pennsylvania Federal painted pine waterbench, 63in. wide. $700

American Victorian walnut hall tree, signed T. Brooks & Co., New York, 36in. wide. $800

American Hepplewhite mahogany washstand, circa 1800, on square tapering legs, 14½in. square. $850

Queen Anne mahogany dumb waiter with three shelves, diam. 24in. $900

Satinwood dumb waiter with circular top and four further trays, circa 1900, 22in. diam. $905

Early 19th century William IV rosewood canterbury, 20in. wide. $1,250

AMERICANA

STANDS

Early 19th century American country Federal washstand, 18in. wide. $1,400

Mid 18th century mahogany jardiniere, 28¾in. high. $1,465

Rococo revival walnut etagere, American, circa 1865, with pierced, carved crest, 45½in. wide. $1,500

Two-tiered rosewood jardiniere stand, circa 1895, 16in. square. $1,880

Early 19th century Regency black-painted and gilded canterbury, 23in. wide. $2,500

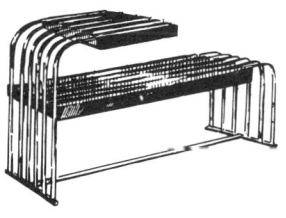

Art Deco chrome and mirror coat-rack with umbrella stand, circa 1925. $2,590

AMERICANA

STOOLS

19th century French Empire style banquette in mahogany with upholstered seat, 32in. wide. $750

One of a pair of Queen Anne footstools, circa 1750, 18in. wide. $1,800

American William and Mary joint stool, circa 1700, 26in. wide, on stretcher base. $3,000

Early 19th century window seat in the manner of Duncan Phyfe. $3,940

Queen Anne walnut stool, seat covered in gros and petit-point needlework, 19in. diam. $4,285

Queen Anne walnut stool on cabriole legs edged with C-scrolls, 22½in. wide. $6,000

AMERICANA

SUITES

Art Deco three-piece suite, 1930's, in cut velvet. $655

American 20th century walnut parlor set of two pieces. $750

Part of a custom mahogany Jacobean style set of twelve dining chairs.
$1,000

AMERICANA

SUITES

Two-piece Art Nouveau carved mahogany suite with carved backs and arms, settee 49in. long. $1,000

A 1930's tubular steel three-piece suite. $1,015

A three-piece Renaissance revival parlor set, Eastern United States. $1,200

AMERICANA

SUITES

American Victorian incised walnut and burl veneer parlor set of a sofa and two chairs, circa 1870. $1,200

A four-piece suite of cast iron garden furniture, late 19th century. $1,250

Victorian Eastlake walnut and burl veneer parlor set with cartouche carved crest. $1,300

AMERICANA
SUITES

Victorian carved walnut parlor set of seven pieces. $1,800

A Victorian carved walnut three-piece Renaissance revival suite. $1,900

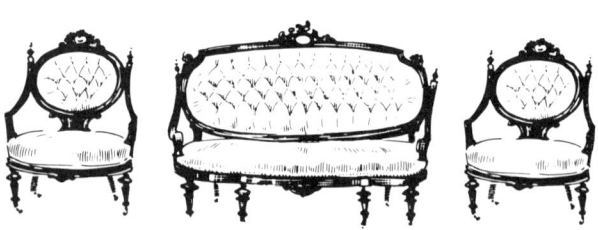

Part of an American six-piece Victorian Renaissance revival rosewood parlor set, circa 1860. $2,300

AMERICANA

SUITES

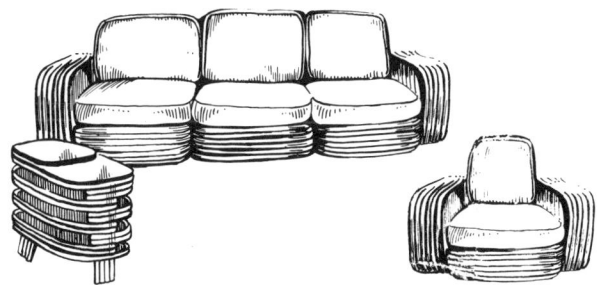

Part of a fourteen-piece set of bamboo porch furniture, circa 1940. $3,500

Suite of Art Nouveau walnut seat furniture, circa 1900, 48in. wide.
$3,940

Part of a four-piece walnut drawingroom suite, circa 1860, in gold upholstery.
$4,245

AMERICANA

SUITES

Part of a Victorian nine-piece suite in walnut. $5,400

Part of an eleven-piece suite of bamboo porch funiture, circa 1930, 30in. high. $5,900

Victorian suite of sofa and two chairs in rosewood with velvet upholstery. $51,750

AMERICANA

TABLES

20th century American Chippendale style pie crust tip table, top with carved edge, 30in. diam. $225

Limbert oak library table, Holland, Michigan, circa 1906, 48in. wide. $250

Victorian walnut turtle top table with white marble top. $300

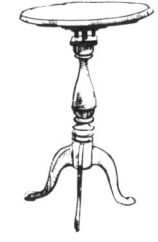

American walnut tilt-top birdcage table, 18½in. diam. $325

19th century American Greco-Roman revival walnut marble top table, 41in. long. $350

Late 19th century American rococo revival rosewood marble top table, 34in. wide. $400

AMERICANA

TABLES

George II mahogany dumb waiter, 24in. diam. $450

19th century Regency drum table with marquetry inlay, 25in. diam. $450

Victorian walnut table with round marble top inlaid with intricate patterns. $550

Mid 19th century black painted and gilded low table, 18in. wide. $600

Pietra Dura top table on central column, 30½in. high. $600

Round walnut dining table with carved legs and stretchers, sold with six matching chairs. $650

AMERICANA

TABLES

Mid 19th century American pitch pine refectory table, 96½in. long. $745

Victorian oak library table with leather top, American, 19th century, 38in. wide. $775

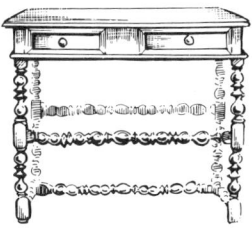

Late 17th/early 18th century William and Mary one-drawer table on turned legs, 29¼in. wide. $800

19th century Regency tilt-top breakfast table in mahogany, 59in. long. $850

Art Nouveau tripod shaped occasional table, inlaid with marquetry. $1,100

Onyx and ormolu three-tiered table, circa 1891, 31in. high. $1,400

AMERICANA

TABLES

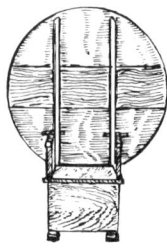

18th century American country pine chair table with circular top, 46in. diam. $1,400

17th century Provincial oak draw table on ring turned legs, 50in. wide. $1,550

Federal cherrywood banquet table, circa 1810, on ten turned and spiral legs, 81in. long. $1,650

Mahogany dining table with two D-ends, circa 1870, 108in. wide, extended. $1,700

Early 19th century Regency penwork sewing table, 20in. wide. $1,750

Early 19th century painted maple and pine hutch table, 41in. diam. $1,900

AMERICANA

TABLES

American mahogany dining table and set of chairs, circa 1900. $2,500

Important Victorian walnut Eastlake style library table with red marble inset, 51in. wide. $3,600

Early 18th century George II mahogany triple top games table, 33¼in. wide. $5,000

A kidney-shaped table, sold with two chairs. $5,625

Early 19th century Regency mahogany games table, 54¼in. wide. $5,625

One of a pair of rare New York City Empire rosewood and grain painted games tables, 36½in. wide. $10,500

AMERICANA

CARD TABLES

20th century American, Federal style mahogany card table with shaped top, 35in. wide. $350

American Victorian Renaissance revival walnut games table, 36½in. wide, circa 1865. $350

Federal mahogany card table with demi-lune top on square tapered legs, 35in. wide. $400

American Greco-Roman revival mahogany games table, circa 1820, 36in. wide. $500

Federal mahogany demi-lune card table, New England, circa 1800, 35½in. wide. $600

Federal mahogany card table, circa 1795, 36in. wide. $700

AMERICANA

CARD TABLES

American Federal mahogany card table, circa 1810, with shaped top above satinwood skirt, 35½in. wide. $800

Federal cherrywood card table, New England, circa 1810, 34½in. wide. $900

American Queen Anne card table, circa 1765, with mahogany top, 32½in. wide. $1,000

New England Federal mahogany inlaid card table, top with ovolu corners, circa 1700, 34¾in. wide. $1,600

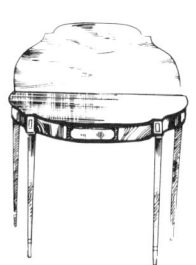

Rare Federal mahogany inlaid card table, Massachusetts, circa 1790, 36in. wide. $2,600

American Federal mahogany and mahogany veneer card table with shaped top, 36in. wide, circa 1810. $2,900

AMERICANA

CARD TABLES

Federal mahogany card table by John and Thomas Seymour, Massachusetts, circa 1795, 35½in. square. $3,100

American Federal mahogany card table with swell front, circa 1795, 36½in. square. $3,600

Fine Sheraton mahogany and branch satinwood card table, 35½in. wide, circa 1800. $4,000

Federal mahogany card table, Boston, Massachusetts, circa 1810, 37in. wide. $4,250

George II walnut card table with squared outset corners, 34in. wide. $6,000

Chippendale mahogany games table, Boston, circa 1760, 33½in. wide. $21,000

AMERICANA

CONSOL TABLES

20th century American Federal style mahogany consol table with inlaid edge, 35in. wide. $125

New England Victorian walnut turtle top table, circa 1870, 37in. wide. $850

20th century American Chippendale style mahogany marble top table, 60in. wide. $1,200

Early 18th century George I giltwood consol table, 48in. wide. $1,855

One of a pair of George III consol tables in satinwood veneers, 33in. long. $2,400

Fine lacquered wood and chrome consol table by Donald Desky, circa 1927, 72in. wide. $5,625

AMERICANA

DRESSING TABLES

Rococo revival walnut mirrored bureau, circa 1860, with arched top mirror, 47½in. $475

American rococo revival rosewood and rosewood veneer dressing table, circa 1860, 24½in. wide. $600

Renaissance revival walnut and burl veneer princess bureau with carved crest, circa 1870, 63½in. wide. $950

Antique rosewood marble top dresser with oval mirror, stretcher with urn finial, 43½in. wide. $1,300

Hepplewhite inlaid mahogany Beau Brummel dressing table, with satinwood line inlay, 32½in. wide. $1,400

Part of a late 19th century American bamboo turned maple and maple veneer bedroom set. $5,000

AMERICANA

DROP-LEAF TABLES

American custom oak gateleg table, circa 1920, 43 x 40in. $375

American Chippendale walnut drop-leaf table on cabriole legs, 48in. wide, open. $950

Gustav Stickley oak drop-leaf table, circa 1909, 32in. diam., open. $1,100

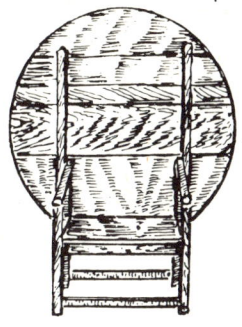

18th century American pine and maple chair table with circular top, 47in. diam. $1,150

Mid 18th century New England country Queen Anne cherry and hickory butterfly table, 40in. wide. $1,200

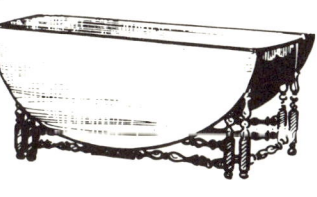

Jacobean style oak gateleg table on turned and blocked legs and stretchers, 60in. wide, open. $1,200

AMERICANA

DROP-LEAF TABLES

Cherrywood inlaid dining table with drop-leaves, circa 1790, 48in. wide. $1,800

Queen Anne cherrywood dining table, Connecticut, circa 1760, 42½in. wide. $2,100

William and Mary maple and cherry butterfly table, New England, circa 1730, 44in. wide. $2,200

American Chippendale mahogany drop-leaf table, 48in. wide, circa 1755. $3,000

18th century George III walnut gate-leg table on block and baluster turned supports, 30in. wide. $3,000

Queen Anne mahogany drop-leaf dining table, 48in. wide. $3,000

AMERICANA

DROP-LEAF TABLES

Early 19th century Shaker cherrywood drop-leaf table, 29in. wide. $3,000

American William and Mary maple gateleg table, circa 1700, with reel turned legs, 48in. wide. $3,750

Early 18th century William and Mary butterfly table, 38½in. diam. $3,970

New England William and Mary maple and cherrywood butterfly table, circa 1720, 36in. wide. $4,250

Federal painted harvest table, New England, circa 1810, 72in. long. $4,725

Queen Anne maple drop-leaf dining table, 36in. diam., on cabriole legs. $5,700

AMERICANA

PEMBROKE TABLES

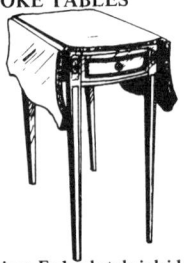

American Federal style inlaid mahogany Pembroke table with shaped top and leaves, circa 1920, 31in. wide. $225

American Sheraton inlaid mahogany night table, circa 1800, with square top, 32½in. high. $325

One of a pair of Custom Hepplewhite tiger maple and mahogany veneer Pembroke tables, American, 20th century, 36in. wide. $450

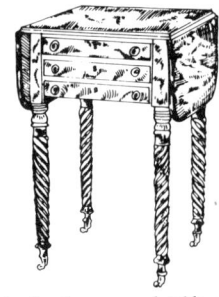

Federal mahogany work table, American, circa 1800, 36¼in. high, on four turned and rope carved legs. $500

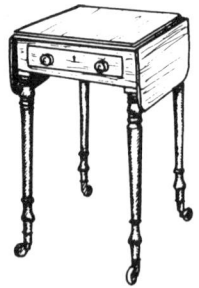

Late Georgian mahogany Pembroke table with two-flap top, 34in. wide, extended. $625

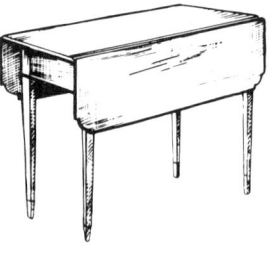

Late 18th century cherrywood inlaid Pembroke table, American, 36in. wide. $900

AMERICANA

PEMBROKE TABLES

American Federal mahogany Pembroke table, top with rounded corners, circa 1795, 39in. wide. $950

American walnut Pembroke table, Pennsylvania, circa 1790, 39in. wide, open. $1,300

Late 19th century Federal mahogany Pembroke table on square tapering legs, 39½in. wide. $1,400

Early 19th century George III faded rosewood Pembroke table, 41¾in. wide. $2,000

George III mahogany Pembroke table with serpentine top crossbanded with satinwood, 41½in. wide. $2,000

One of a pair of Federal mahogany Pembroke tables, circa 1808-16, 39¾in. wide. $7,000

AMERICANA

TAVERN TABLES

William and Mary style birch tavern table, circa 1930, 50in. wide. $350

18th century American tavern table with oval top and vase and ring turned legs, 34in. wide. $550

William and Mary maple and pine tavern table, circa 1750, 31in. wide. $850

Early 18th century William and Mary tavern table in walnut, Pennsylvania, 40in. wide. $1,000

Early 18th century William and Mary maple and pine tavern table, 40in. wide, New England. $1,800

William and Mary style tavern table, circa 1700-30, 37in. wide. $2,000

AMERICANA

TEA TABLES

Mid 18th century American Queen Anne tea table, 25½in. high. $250

Late 19th century American Victorian rosewood tilt-top tea table, 19in. diam. $450

Late 18th century George III tea table with pie crust top, 26in. diam. $650

Federal mahogany tip table, New England, circa 1790, 28¼in. high. $675

18th century provincial painted table with single gate, 42in. long. $850

Chippendale mahogany tilt-top tea table, with square top, circa 1760, 44in. $850

AMERICANA

TEA TABLES

Chippendale mahogany tilt-top tea table with circular top, circa 1755, 33½in. diam. $950

American Queen Anne maple tea table with tapering round legs on pad feet, 34in. wide. $1,000

Late 18th century Chippendale mahogany tea table, New England, 44in. square. $1,000

Limbert oval oak table with cut-out stretcher, 36in. wide. $1,150

American Queen Anne cherrywood tea table with applied molded edge, 29½in. wide. $1,700

Queen Anne oval top table, New England, circa 1794, 39¼in. wide. $4,800

AMERICANA

WORK TABLES

Late 19th century Renaissance revival walnut and burl veneer sewing table, 21in. wide. $600

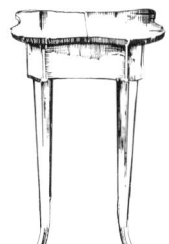

Northern New England Federal birch work table, circa 1800, 19in. wide. $755

19th century Regency bow-fronted sewing table in mahogany and mahogany veneer, 36in. wide. $900

American Federal mahogany work table, Boston, circa 1810, 27½in. wide, drawers with ivory knobs. $1,900

18th century George III sewing table in rosewood, burl and other veneers, with hinged lid, 18¾in. wide. $1,900

Federal tiger maple astragal end work table, New York, circa 1800, 29½in. wide. $3,000

AMERICANA

GLASS BOTTLES

Amber glass 'Hair Tonic' bottle. $9

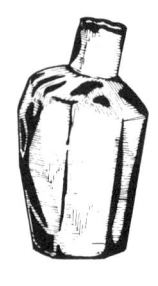

Victorian octagonal glass ink bottle. $15

A 20th century midwife's glass medical bottle, 4¾in. high, in chromium plated holder. $35

Red glass Barrel Bitters bottle, American, circa 1860-80, 9¼in. high. $40

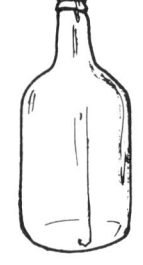

Early 19th century green wine bottle, 13in. tall. $40

Amber glass Indian Queen Bitters bottle, circa 1870-80, 12¼in. high. $50

Birdcage ink bottle on square base, in pale green glass, 3¼in. high, circa 1860-90. $50

Green blown glass bottle with etched decoration and dated 1829, 30cm. high. $125

Mid 19th century pressed amber glass Bitters bottle by A. M. Bininger & Co., 32cm. high. $180

AMERICANA

GLASS BOTTLES

Pressed glass cologne bottle, Sandwich, Massachusetts, circa 1840, 6½in. high. $200

American blown three-mold bottle in olive green glass, circa 1830, 17cm. high. $275

Heavily swirled glass brandy bar bottle in emerald green, 27.5cm. high, circa 1840-60. $290

Early 19th century American blown three-mold aqua bottle, 21cm. high. $350

One of a pair of pressed glass bar bottles with flared bases, Sandwich, Massachusetts, 10in. high, circa 1850. $425

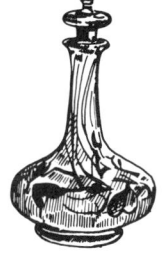

Tiffany iridescent glass perfume bottle and stopper, circa 1900, 11.5cm. high. $700

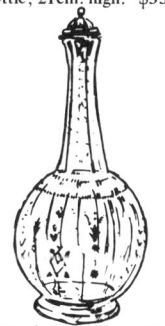

One of a set of four gilt toilet bottles, 20cm. high, circa 1830, with matching stoppers. $785

Blown-in mold bottle in green color, New England, circa 1825, 6¼in. high. $900

Tiffany green ground bottle, circa 1905. $6,190

AMERICANA

GLASS BOWLS

Tiffany Favrile glass bowl, 26cm. diam., slightly cracked. $120

Findlay onyx opalescent covered sugar bowl, circa 1890, Ohio, 5¾in. high. $175

Late 19th century Eastern United States two-colored cut glass compote, 6in. diam. $175

American cut glass Monteith bowl, circa 1880, 10in. diam. $225

19th century Eastern United States three-color cut glass bowl, 5in. diam. $225

Early 20th century Tiffany Favrile blue iridescent glass bowl, New York. $300

Wheeling peachblow rosebowl, 5½in. high. $300

Late 19th century intaglio and cut glass bowl by Pitkin & Brooks, 7¾in. diam. $325

AMERICANA

GLASS BOWLS

Early 20th century Northwood purple bowl and stand with six cups, 10¾in. high. $350

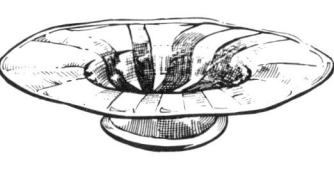

Tiffany Favrile pastel glass compote, New York, circa 1910, 16in. diam. $350

Mt. Washington cameo glass bowl, late 19th century, in opaque pink on white, 9in. diam. $375

Northwood purple carnival glass punchbowl and stand with cups, Ohio, circa 1910, 10in. high. $400

Early 20th century iridescent glass bowl, marked Quezal, New York, 13cm. diam. $400

Late 19th century New England amberina compote on pedestal base, 9in. diam. $425

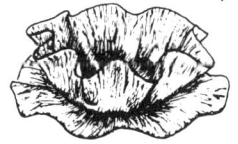

One of a pair of early 20th century Tiffany Favrile glass finger bowls, with undertrays. $425

One of a set of three Tiffany iridescent glass finger bowls, circa 1900, 12cm. diam. $440

AMERICANA

GLASS BOWLS

Hawkes cut glass fruit bowl, Corning, New York, circa 1900, 12in. diam. $450

Tiffany blue iridescent bowl with swirled blown out body. $450

Large early 20th century Sinclaire & Co. intaglio cut fruit bowl, Corning, New York. $500

Antique American brilliant cut punch-bowl, 34.6cm. diam. $530

Iridescent blue Favrile glass flower center by Tiffany & Co., early 20th century, 11in. diam. $550

Late 19th century Tiffany & Co. standing fruit bowl, New York, 10¼in. diam., 28 Troy oz. $600

Pressed glass miniature covered tureen, Sandwich, Massachusetts, circa 1838, 3in. long. $600

Iridescent Favrile glass flower bowl, by Tiffany, 13in. diam. $640

AMERICANA

GLASS BOWLS

One of nine Steuben Rosaline cased bowls, New York, circa 1925, signed, 5in. diam. $650

One of a pair of American glass compotes, circa 1845, with pointed scalloped rims, 4¾in. high. $750

Golden iridescent Favrile glass rose bowl by Tiffany Studios, 25cm. diam. $820

A Tiffany Favrile golden iridescent bowl with globular body, 19cm. high. $875

Late 19th century Eastern United States cut glass two-part punchbowl, 14in. diam. $1,000

One of a set of six Tiffany iridescent glass bowls and saucers, circa 1900, 6cm. high. $1,700

Early 19th century American expanding dip mold amber glass bowl, 20cm. diam. $1,900

Rare mounted cameo glass wall flower bowl, 13in. diam. $2,140

AMERICANA

GLASS CANDLESTICKS

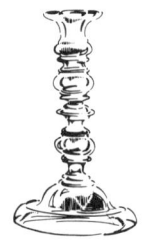

Freeblown glass candlestick, Massachusetts, circa 1860, 8½in. high. $220

Early 20th century Aurene candlestick, signed, 10in. high. $225

Late 18th century freeblown glass pricket candlestick, 9in. high. $275

One of a pair of Canary dolphin glass candlesticks, with petal rim cup, circa 1845, 25cm. high. $300

One of a pair of early 20th century Tiffany Favrile glass candlesticks, New York, 7¼in. high. $400

One of a pair of powder blue glass candlesticks, circa 1835, 17.5cm. high. $400

Bronze and Favrile glass candlestick, by Tiffany, 8in. high. $605

Tiffany bronze two-light chamberstick with blown-out green glass holders, 15cm. high. $700

One of a pair of cobalt blue glass candlesticks, Massachusetts, circa 1840, 9½in. high. $700

AMERICANA

GLASS CANDLESTICKS

One of a pair of pressed glass candlesticks, Sandwich, Massachusetts, 1835-45, 7½in. high. $725

Pressed glass candlestick, Sandwich, Massachusetts, 1830-35, 6in. high. $825

Pressed glass candlestick in cobalt blue, Sandwich, Massachusetts, 1830-35, 5½in. high. $850

CUPS & MUGS

19th century Mary Gregory beaker depicting a young girl. $90

New England peachblow punch cup with ribbed handle, 2¼in. high. $175

One of a set of four Tiffany iridescent glass mugs, circa 1900, 6.5cm. high. $475

Agate peachblow punch cup by the New England Glass Co., circa 1887, 2½in. high. $600

Tiffany gold iridescent loving cup with three handles, 5in. high. $820

Late 19th century plated amberina punch cup, ribbed, with shaped rim, 2¾in. high. $1,300

AMERICANA

GLASS DECANTERS

Art Deco mallet-shaped decanter. $55

An Art Deco Bristol glass and metal decanter set, Eastern United States, circa 1927. $100

Blown Masonic clear glass decanter with fluted bottom border, 28cm. high. $175

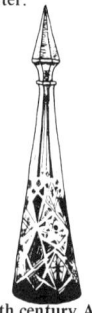

Late 19th century American two-color green cut glass decanter of conical shape, 16¾in. high. $200

Cobalt blue bar bottle, cork stopper with pewter and cobalt stopper, circa 1850, 12in. high. $250

Miniature freeblown glass decanter and stopper, circa 1830, Sandwich, Massachusetts, 3½in. high. $275

One of four glass Horn of Plenty decanters, American, circa 1850. $350

Part of a twenty-eight-piece crystal cordial and wine set, circa 1870, initialed RSSA. $350

Blown three mold miniature decanter, Sandwich, Massachusetts, circa 1828, 3½in. high. $450

AMERICANA

GLASS DISHES

Late 19th century Eastern United States cut glass dish in cornucopia and crosshatch patterns. $225

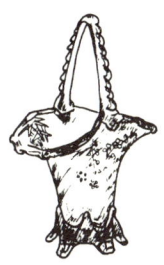

Late 19th century amberina basket, floral decorated, 10½in. high. $275

Late 19th century amberina glass overshot basket with looped handle, 12.5cm. high. $325

Late 19th century Eastern United States two-color cut glass wine glass, 4½in. high. $325

Late 19th century Tuthill cut glass dish, signed, Middletown, New York, 8¾in. long. $350

WMF electroplated dessert dish stand with cut glass bowl, circa 1900, 42.5cm. high. $450

Tiffany bronze and gold iridescent bride's basket, 7½in. high. $475

Cameo glass bride's basket by Mount Washington Glass Co. $750

Early 20th century Libbey Glass salesman sample, cut glass plate, Toledo, Ohio, 6in. diam. $1,200

AMERICANA

GLASS JUGS

Cut glass footed creamer by T. G. Hawkes & Co., New York, circa 1900, 6in. high. $110

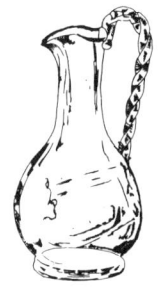

Early 19th century glass champagne jug with trefoil rim, diagonal ice funnel, 11½in. diam. $140

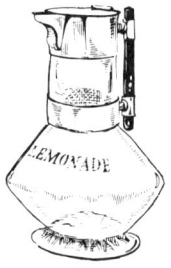

Plated metal and glass lemonade jug, engraved, 22cm. with ebonized wooden handle. $145

Pressed glass water pitcher with applied handle, 9¼in. high. $150

19th century American amberina conical water pitcher, 8½in. high. $175

Glass water pitcher by Hawkes, Corning, New York, circa 1900, 8½in. high. $200

Eastern United States cut glass footed pitcher with paneled pouring spout, circa 1880, 9in. high. $200

One of a pair of blue glass ewer ornaments decorated by Mary Gregory, 43cm. high. $205

American cut glass champagne jug, circa 1890, 13½in. high with flared rim. $300

AMERICANA

GLASS JUGS

Glass lemonade jug with electroplated mounts, 1880's, 22.25cm. high. $310

Blown glass water pitcher by Thomas Caines, South Boston Glass Co., circa 1815, 6¾in. high. $350

Blown three-mold glass jug with wide flaring rim and pouring spout, circa 1828, 6¼in. high. $425

American three-mold cobalt blue cream jug, circa 1830, 11.5cm. high. $475

Late 19th century Eastern United States cut glass water pitcher, 14½in. high. $575

Cased wheeling peach blow pitcher, 5½in. high. $650

Late 19th century cut glass water pitcher, Eastern United States, 6½in. high, with saw-tooth rim. $700

Unusual glass jug of urn shape, circa 1820, 29cm. high. $745

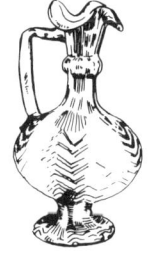

Rainbow satin glass ewer in herringbone pattern with mother-of-pearl finish, 10in. high. $950

AMERICANA

GLASS MISCELLANEOUS

Late 19th century American papier mache and mother-of-pearl castor set. $150

Early 20th century Tiffany gold iridescent pepper shaker, New York, 2¾in. high. $150

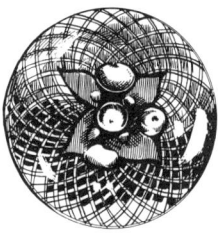

Mid 19th century New England fruit paperweight, Massachusetts, 2¾in. diam. $175

American Gothic revival walnut and glass terrarium with peaked top, 29½in. wide, circa 1840. $200

Molded glass pomade jar in the form of a bear, Sandwich, Massachusetts, circa 1845, 3¾in. high. $200

Smith Brothers powder jar with opal glass body and plated silver top. $225

American amberina castor set, circa 1890, in plated silver frame. $350

Late 19th century Eastern United States cut glass flower center in Harvard pattern, 7½in. diam. $375

18th century oak and maple hour glass, New England, 8in. high. $400

AMERICANA

GLASS MISCELLANEOUS

Late 19th century stained glass panel, Boston, signed W. J. McPherson, Boston, 15¼in. high. $425

One of a pair of cut glass candelabra, circa 1900, 25½in. high. $450

20th century Tuthill glass tray, signed, 13½in. long. $525

Albertine covered jar, New Bedford, Massachusetts, circa 1885. $525

Early 20th century Burmese double-handled urn by Mt. Washington Glass Co., Massa., 13½in. high. $675

American black wooden butler holding a rack with glasses, circa 1900, 48cm. high. $1,100

A scent bottle, by Tiffany. $1,575

American flower weight cut with circular windows, in pink, white and green, 8.2cm. diam. $1,750

Mt. Washington Royal Flemish covered jar, 7in. high. $2,400

AMERICANA

GLASS VASES

Early 20th century Wave Crest opalene glass vase by C. F. Monroe Co., Meriden, Connecticut. $90

19th century American amberina vase of baluster shape, 9¾in. high. $100

Late 19th century Eastern United States cut glass vase, 10in. high. $155

Late 19th century Eastern United States three-branch cranberry glass epergne, 20½in. high. $175

Satin glass mother-of-pearl vase, America, circa 1880, 7in. high. $175

Coralene and Rubina glass vase with flared neck, late 19th century, America, 7¾in. high. $200

Late 19th century Mount Washington decorated Jack-in-the-Pulpit vase, New Bedford. $200

Late 19th century American cranberry overlay cut glass vase with scalloped top, 10in. high. $200

Late 19th century peach-blow vase with coral decoration, 12in. high. $250

AMERICANA

GLASS VASES

Wheeling peachblow vase, West Virginia, circa 1890, 8¾in. high. $275

Late 19th century cut glass flower vase, American, 20cm. high. $300

Amberina glass vase with bulbous body, circa 1890, 18cm. high. $300

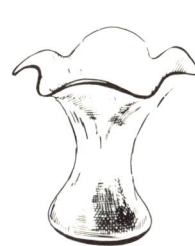

American gold iridescent Art glass vase, signed Aurene 729, circa 1900. $300

Eastern United States tall cut glass vase with ruffled rim, circa 1890, 16in. high. $325

Late 19th century miniature Tiffany blue iridescent vase of baluster form, 2¾in. high, signed. $350

Early 20th century Tiffany Favrile iridescent gold vase, New York, 5½in. high. $375

Tiffany iridescent glass vase, 9.5cm. high, 1912. $385

Handel cameo glass vase, circa 1920, signed Mosher, 9¾in. high. $400

AMERICANA

GLASS VASES

Pressed glass vase in canary yellow, Sandwich, Massachusetts, circa 1840, 5¾in. high. $425

Early 20th century gold iridescent vase by Tiffany, New York, 3½in. high. $425

Tiffany gold/blue iridescent Favrile glass vase with flaring neck, early 20th century, 22cm. high. $475

Free-form Art glass vase, by Tiffany on dome foot, 26cm. high. $500

Early 20th century Quezal iridescent Art Glass vase, New York, 12½in. high. $550

Early 20th century Tiffany blue/purple iridescent Favrile glass vase, 30cm. high. $550

New England peachblow lily form vase, 18in. high. $600

Pressed glass vase in emerald green, Sandwich, Massachusetts, 1835-40, 10in. high. $600

Tiffany trumpet-shaped glass vase on domed foot, 37.5cm. high. $650

AMERICANA

GLASS VASES

One of a pair of amethyst tulip glasses with scalloped rims, circa 1845, 10in. high. $725

Late 19th century Burmese glass vase, New Bedford, Massachusetts, 11¾in. high. $750

Moss agate vase by Steuben, Corning, New York, circa 1920, 10¾in. high. $800

Tiffany iridescent glass spill vase with gilt bronze foot, circa 1900, 34.25cm. high. $820

Early 19th century American footed Hawkes cut glass vase, 20in. high. $900

One of a pair of American Libbey amberina Art glass vases, circa 1900, 9in. high. $950

A Tiffany Favrile turquoise iridescent vase with oviform body, 13.5cm. high. $970

Late 19th century blue iridescent glass vase by Tiffany, New York, 11¾in. high. $975

Early 20th century Tiffany Favrile glass floriform vase, New York, 10¾in. high. $1,000

AMERICANA

GLASS VASES

Early 20th century etched and cut glass vase with flaring top and bottom.
$1,150

Late 19th century Tiffany Favrile gold iridescent vase, New York, with rolled neck, 6¾in. high.
$1,150

Burmese glass vase, labeled Mount Washington Glass Co., circa 1890, 11¾in. high. $1,150

Late 19th century Mount Washington Burmese stick vase, 29cm. high. $1,350

Royal Flemish vase in mustard yellow with ruffled rim, circa 1889.
$1,400

Royal Flemish glass modified stick vase, circa 1889, 33cm. high. $1,500

Tiffany flower form vase with green and white flower, 11¾in. high.
$1,530

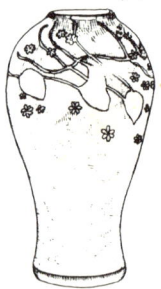

Tiffany Favrile iridescent millefiori oviform vase, 6in. high. $1,620

Blue aurene decorated vase by Steuben Glass Works, Corning, New York, circa 1905, 6¾in. high.
$1,700

AMERICANA

GLASS VASES

A Tiffany Cypriot vase. $2,250

Tiffany iridescent glass vase, 18cm. high, 1914. $2,310

Rare Mount Washington peachblow vase with scalloped rim, New England, circa 1890, 4¼in. high. $2,500

Two-color cameo vase, circa 1880, in opaque white cut to blue, 10in. high. $3,200

Tiffany paperweight aquamarine vase, New York, circa 1910, 5in. diam. $3,500

Late 19th century Tiffany Favrile paperweight vase, New York, 6in. high. $3,700

Tiffany flower vase of milky tone, 44cm. high. $4,050

Gold and yellow iridescent vase, by Louis C. Tiffany, 38cm. high, circa 1900. $6,075

A rare Jack-in-the-Pulpit Tiffany peacock iridescent glass vase, 1900. $11,250

AMERICANA

GLASS WINDOWS

Late 18th century architectural lunette window, 94in. long. $850

Art Deco cameo and stained glass window, circa 1930, 49½in. long. $1,300

A triptych stained glass landscape window, circa 1905. $3,715

A triptych stained glass thistle window by Tiffany, circa 1904, 36in. wide. $2,475

AMERICANA

WINE GLASSES

One of ten American cut glass wine glasses with knopped stems, circa 1910, 4in. high. $75

Rare late 19th century unsigned Dorflinger two-color cut glass wine glass, Eastern United States, 4½in. high. $150

One of six late 19th century American green overlay cut glass liqueur glasses, 5¼in. high, on long stems. $175

One of four late 19th century American two-color cranberry cut glass wine glasses, 5in. high. $250

One of two 18th century freeblown airtwist wine glasses, 7in. high. $250

One of six early 20th century American cut glass goblets, with starburst bases, 6in. high. $400

One of four early 20th century Tiffany iridescent gold glass goblets, 5¾in. high. $475

One of a set of twelve late 19th century two-color brilliant cut champagne glasses, American, 4½in. high. $600

One of a set of four Tiffany Favrile glass wine glasses, signed, 19.5cm. $965

AMERICANA

GRAMOPHONES

Columbia type BVT graphophone, circa 1908, American. $300

Columbia AA graphophone, American, circa 1906. $350

Early 20th century table gramophone with metal horn. $425

Columbia model AA graphophone with two-minute gearing, American, circa 1902-1904. $500

Columbia AJ disk graphophone with 7in. turntable, circa 1902, complete with original case. $510

American Columbia AH disk gramophone with large conical black horn and brass bell, circa 1904. $690

AMERICANA

GRAMOPHONES

Good Gramophone & Typewriter Co. Junior Monarch gramophone, circa 1908. $735

Gramophone Company, style No. 5 trademark gramophone, in original leather carrying case, circa 1900. $1,010

Gramophone & Typewriter Co., style No. 6, gramophone. $1,055

Fine Gramophone & Typewriter Ltd. senior monarch gramophone, circa 1908. $2,000

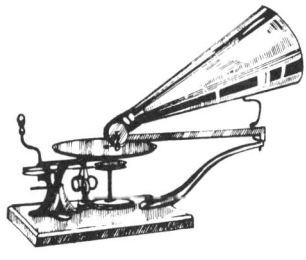

A Gramophone company hand-driven style No. 2 gramophone with 7in. diam. turntable, 1898-1901. $2,500

Gramophone & Typewriter Ltd. New Melba gramophone in mahogany case with mahogany horn. $3,150

AMERICANA

INSTRUMENTS

Nickel and steel American instrument with ebonite handle, 1905, 4¾in. long. $40

American Simplex Model D typewriter in original cardboard box, 1930's, 8¾in. wide. $85

All brass horse-hair singer, 13¼in. long, circa 1860. $100

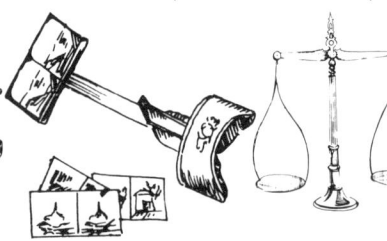
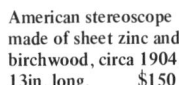

Eastman Studio scale by Kodak, New York, 9in. wide. $100

American stereoscope made of sheet zinc and birchwood, circa 1904, 13in. long. $150

Late 19th century American double pan scales with knife blade balance, 75cm. high. $240

Mid 19th century American brass Altizimuth theodolite by N. & L. E. Gurley, 1ft. high. $350

Lambert typewriter by Gramophone & Typewriter Ltd., circa 1900. $450

American rare and interesting radio in the form of a Coca-Cola bottle, 24in. high, circa 1930. $450

AMERICANA

INSTRUMENTS

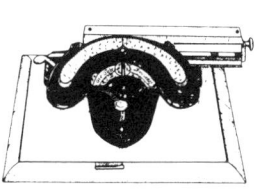
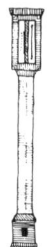
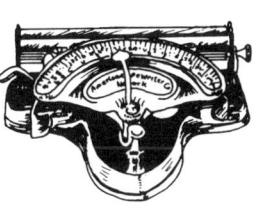

American Globe typewriter by the American Typewriter Co., circa 1895. $510

Mid 19th century stick barometer by D. E. Lent, Rochester, New York, 37¾in. high. $525

American typewriter by The American Typewriter Co., circa 1895, 25cm. wide. $525

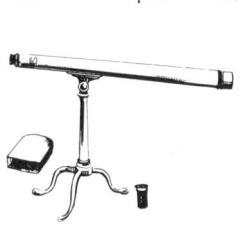

Brass telescope, stand and case by C. G. King, Boston, circa 1845. $700

Double column barometer marked H. A. Clum, Rochester, New York, circa 1860, 37½in. high. $800

American typewriter by Merritt, No. 12095, 12¼in. wide, circa 1895, on oak base. $1,015

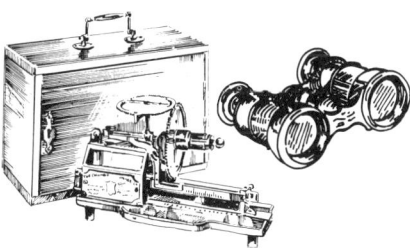

Rare Victor typewriter, American, circa 1895, 12in. wide. $1,485

Columbia typewriter No. 2, circa 1885, in original wooden carrying case. $2,760

Opera glasses used by Abraham Lincoln on the night of his assassination. $23,650

AMERICANA

IRON & TIN

One of two early 19th century tin candle molds, 13½in. $75

Late 18th century American wrought iron skillet with rat-tail handle, 33¼in. long. $125

17th century iron pan lamp, with ramshorn screw attaching tripod base, 13in. $150

Early 19th century American cast-iron tilting kettle, 14in. high. $175

19th century New England tin Canada goose decoy, painted dark gray, 21½in. long. $200

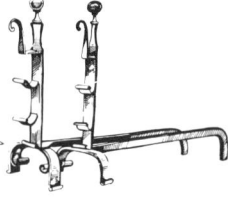

18th century American wrought iron andirons, with brass ball finials, 26in. high. $225

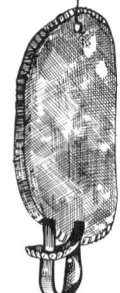

19th century American tin wall sconce with fluted border, 15in. high. $275

Late 19th century cast iron Victorian doll's house fencing, 6in. long, four sections. $275

17th century iron pan lamp. $300

AMERICANA

IRON & TIN

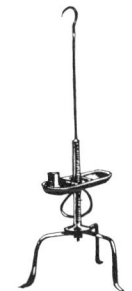

17th century iron pan lamp with wick support and candleholder. $350

Early 18th century American wrought iron pipe kiln, 13½in. long. $350

18th century American iron standing candle holder, 29in. high. $375

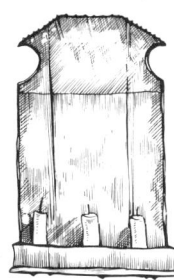

19th century American tin wall sconce with shaped tooled crest, 16½in. high. $375

Polished cast iron American Eagle, circa 1820, 18 x 18in. $400

17th century iron birdcage candleholder on tripod base, 14½in. $675

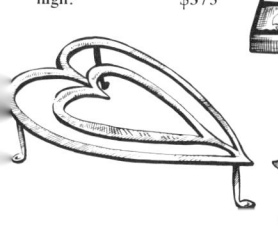

18th century American wrought iron trivet of concentric heart shape. $800

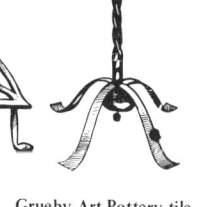

Grueby Art Pottery tile and cast iron table, Boston, Massachusetts, 20th century, 13¼in. wide. $900

Early 18th century standing floor lighting device, 65in. high. $1,600

AMERICANA

JEWELRY

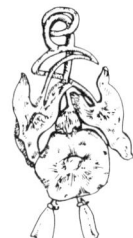

Art Nouveau pearl and enamel pendant, circa 1900, slightly damaged. $90

Georg Jensen brooch in silver colored metal, 6cm. wide, 1920's. $175

Silver gilt and plique-a-jour enamel brooch, circa 1905, 4cm. wide $265

14 karat yellow gold chain, composed of alternating textured arrow and oval links, circa 1900, 22in. long. $275

Snake bracelet in green and white enamel on silver. $300

Victorian gold and enamel bangle bracelet, ½in. wide, 21gm. $300

Opal and 9kt. gold pendant of Art Nouveau style. $385

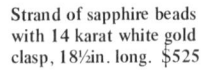

Strand of sapphire beads with 14 karat white gold clasp, 18½in. long. $525

Diamond and platinum bracelet set with sixteen round diamonds. $750

AMERICANA

JEWELRY

Black onyx and diamond ribbon bow brooch by Tiffany & Co. $1,100

Diamond brooch in the form of an inverted crescent, in gold and silver setting. $1,110

Diamond and aquamarine pendant on silver neckchain. $1,150

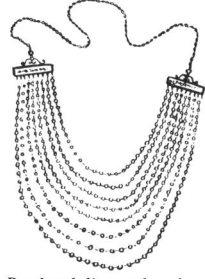

Pearl and diamond necklace of nine strands with cannetille gold clasp. $1,700

Diamond and platinum circle pin set with eighteen round and eighteen baguette diamonds. $1,800

Sapphire and diamond clip of mitre shape, circa 1930, pierced and paveset. $1,900

Diamond brooch designed as a posy of ribbons and flowers, one stone missing. $2,000

Gold buckle by Myer Myers, New York, circa 1765. $10,000

Art Deco sapphire, emerald and diamond brooch, mounted in platinum. $21,375

AMERICANA

JUKE BOXES

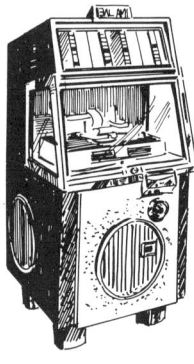

Bal-AMI 45-rpm. juke box, circa 1965, 133cm. high. $250

An American 'AMJ' juke box case, 70in. high, circa 1945-50. $450

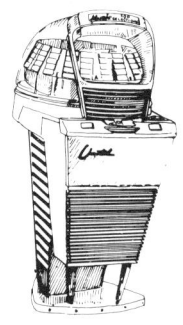

Good Chantel Meteor Musix 200 45-rpm. juke box with large selection of contemporary disks. $1,035

American Wurlitzer 700 78-rpm. juke box in cabinet by Paul Fuller, circa 1939, 4ft. high. $2,760

American Wurlitzer 1100 multi-selector juke box, circa 1947, 4ft.10in. high. $3,700

A fine American Wurlitzer juke box complete with twenty-four records, 1946. $4,000

AMERICANA

LAMP SHADES

20th century painted glass hanging shade. $35

Amberina shade by the New England Glass Co., Massachusetts, circa 1880, 7¼in. diam. $200

Opaque glass lamp shade, 22in. wide, circa 1910. $350

American leaded glass hanging shade, circa 1910 24in. diam. $650

Late 19th century American hanging leaded glass shade, 26¼in. diam. $750

Early 20th century Handel leaded slag glass hanging shade, 22½in. diam., Meriden, Connecticut. $800

Tiffany Studios poinsettia leaded glass shade, domed, circa 1900, 40cm. diam. $3,025

Tiffany pendant colored glass light shade, 28in. diam. $5,625

AMERICANA

LAMPS

Miniature American opaque blue lamp, shade in overlapping leaf motif, circa 1880. $75

20th century American bronze table lamp in the form of a peacock, 16½in. high. $100

Miniature American porcelain lamp with globe-shaped opalescent white shade, circa 1880, 9¼in. high. $125

One of a pair of late 19th/early 20th century brass carriage side lamps, 15in. high. $130

Late 19th century Burmese fairy lamp by Mt. Washington Glass Co., 6in. high. $150

Miniature American cranberry thumbprint lamp with half shade, circa 1880, 7½in. high. $160

American half shade table lamp by Bradley & Hubbard, circa 1870, 20in. high. $180

Miniature American 'Gone with the Wind' lamp with cranberry coin spot shade and font, circa 1880, 8¼in. high. $200

Miniature mauve satin glass lamp with half shade, circa 1880, 7in. high. $225

AMERICANA

LAMPS

Miniature American opalescent 'Gone with the Wind' lamp on square base, circa 1880, 8¼in. high. $230

A large mid 19th century brass ship's lamp, 21in. high. $250

Miniature American satin glass 'Gone with the Wind' lamp, circa 1880, 8½in. high. $250

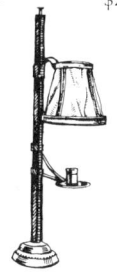

19th century brass and wood candlestick with fabric lamp shade, 24in. $250

Late 19th century American 'Gone with the Wind' lamp on cast brass base, 23½in. high. $300

Art Deco molded glass lamp base in the form of a nude female, 13in. high, circa 1930. $300

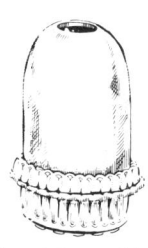

Queen's Burmese fairy lamp by Thos. Webb & Sons, circa 1902, with domed shade, 5¼in. high. $300

Miniature American cranberry glass lamp with molded dot and panel shade and font, circa 1880, 9½in. high. $325

Pairpoint fairy lamp with blown-out pansy shade on wooden base. $325

AMERICANA

LAMPS

Early 19th century free-blown glass whale-oil lamp, 8½in. $350

Astral lamp with brass floral Art Nouveau base and frosted shade. $350

19th century American three-color oil lamp, on milk glass base, 14¾in. high. $350

Art Deco bronze figural table lamp. $355

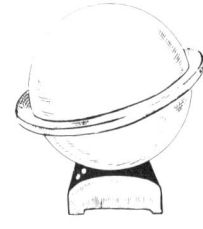

Modernist lamp with spherical green glass shade on blue glass base, 1930's, 31cm. high. $360

One of a pair of early 19th century Regency cut glass candelabra, 9in. high. $370

Handel reverse painted and patinated metal table lamp, Meriden, circa 1930, 20½in. high. $400

Art Deco piano lamp, amber shade with floral motif supported by a bronze nude, on green marble base, circa 1925, 14½in. long. $375

19th century American two-color oil lamp on double step down base, 14¼in. high. $450

AMERICANA

LAMPS

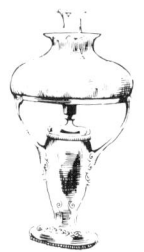

Handel table lamp with open top, Meriden, Connecticut, circa 1910, 19½in. high. $450

American blown glass whale oil lamp, circa 1825, 9¼in. high. $525

Early 20th century Jefferson reverse painted table lamp, 22½in. high. $525

20th century American Jefferson bronzed metal and reverse painted table lamp, 21½in. high. $550

Fulper pottery lamp, Flemington, New Jersey, circa 1900-10. $550

Early 19th century American painted tin and glass whale oil hand lamp, 10¼in. high. $625

Lithophane desk lamp with five panel shade, 15in. high. $650

Webb Burmese fairy lamp with floral decoration, signed. $665

Pairpoint desk lamp with Stratford blown-out shade, 8½in. diam. $750

AMERICANA

LAMPS

Handel table lamp with caramel slag glass paneled shade, Meriden, Connecticut, circa 1915, 23½in. high. $750

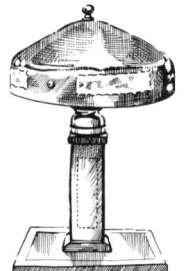

Roycroft patinated hammered copper table lamp, circa 1915, 13¼in. high. $800

Bronze Art Nouveau lamp, circa 1900-10, 52cm. high. $840

Handel bronze patinated metal table lamp with painted glass shade, circa 1910, 53cm. high. $935

Early 20th century Pairpoint bronze and reverse painted table lamp, 23in. high. $1,150

One of a pair of early 19th century marked brass whale oil lamps, American, 7in. high. $1,250

Rare Webb's Burmese glass nightlight stand, circa 1887, 28cm. high. $1,285

Pairpoint table lamp with reverse painted 'Exeter' shade, 22in. high. $1,300

Pairpoint reverse painted glass and brass table lamp with signed shade, circa 1920, 23⅓in. high. $1,500

AMERICANA

LAMPS

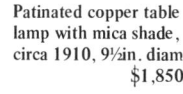

Handel reverse painted glass and bronze table lamp, signed and numbered 6819, circa 1920, 23½in. high. $1,800

Patinated copper table lamp with mica shade, circa 1910, 9½in. diam. $1,850

Handel bronze and reverse painted table lamp, 24½in. high. $1,900

Handel reverse painted glass and bronzed metal table lamp, 18in. high, Meriden, Connecticut, circa 1922. $2,100

Handel reverse painted and painted metal table lamp, no. 712, circa 1920, 23½in. high. $2,400

Handel lamp of tree design, circa 1915, 22in. high. $2,500

Bronze table lamp by Gorham & Co., circa 1900, 58cm. high. $2,810

Glass and wrought iron table lamp, circa 1920, 20¼in. high. $3,250

Cut glass 'Gone with the Wind' lamp, signed L. Straus & Sons, 18½in. high. $6,300

AMERICANA

FLOOR LAMPS

Modernist standard lamp, 1930's, 203cm. high, on spiral glass column. $135

Late 19th century ornate brass and copper tripod telescopic standard lamp. $140

Red painted standard lamp with triangular stem and geometric tripod base, 228.5cm. high. $165

1930's standard lamp, with white glass shade, 188cm. high. $250

20th century brass floorlamp in Art Nouveau style. $270

Art Deco wrought iron standard lamp, 167cm. high, circa 1925. $395

Modernist chromed metal standard lamp with strip light, 1930's, 131.5cm. high. $495

Gustav Stickley mahogany floor lamp, New York, circa 1906, 35in. high. $975

AMERICANA

FLOOR LAMPS

Tiffany Studios gilt bronze reading lamp, 1920's, marked, 135cm. high. $980

Brass and brown aurene floor lamp, 58in. high, circa 1910. $1,100

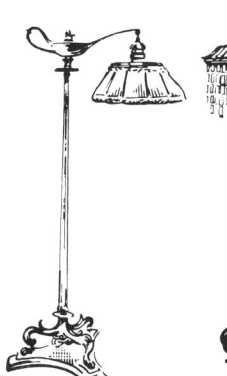

Bronze and Favrile glass linen fold floor lamp, by Tiffany, 55in. high. $1,690

Signed Tiffany bronze floor lamp on slender shaft, shade with opalescent beads. $2,800

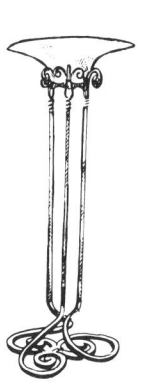

Wrought iron and glass floor lamp, circa 1945, 64½in. high. $2,925

Tiffany leaded Favrile glass and Dore bronze bridge lamp, circa 1900, 57½in. high. $3,200

Favrile glass and bronze bridge floor lamp, by Tiffany, 55½in. high. $3,375

Gilt bronze and Favrile glass twelve-light lily floor lamp, by Tiffany, 55¼in. high. $11,700

AMERICANA

TIFFANY LAMPS

Favrile glass and gilt bronze desk lamp by Tiffany, 9¼in. high. $1,250

Tiffany iridescent Favrile glass and bronze table lamp, New York, circa 1910, 19in. high. $1,350

Bronze Art Nouveau Tiffany Studio lamp. $1,400

One of a pair of late 19th century bronze and Favrile glass candlesticks with shades, by Tiffany Studios, New York, 12in. high. $1,550

Gilt bronze and Favrile glass three-light lily table lamp, by Tiffany, 13in. high. $1,755

Acorn leaded glass and bronze table lamp by Tiffany Studios, 47cm. high. $1,850

One of a pair of iridescent Favrile glass candle lamps, by Tiffany, 14in. high. $2,000

Tiffany Studios bronze lamp base, circa 1910, 57.5cm. high. $2,000

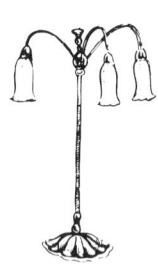

Tiffany bronze three-light table lamp with green, white and gold glass shades, circa 1900. $2,100

AMERICANA

TIFFANY LAMPS

Tiffany 'fabrique' table lamp with ten panel amber linen fold glass shade, 20½in. high. $2,300

Tiffany bronze and Favrile glass three-light lily table lamp, circa 1900, 16in. high. $2,300

Tiffany Studios 'Nautilus' gilt bronze table lamp inset with mother-of-pearl studs, 33.5cm. high. $2,505

A Tiffany peacock feather leaded glass and gilt metal table lamp, 56cm. high. $2,700

Tiffany Studios bronze table lamp with leaded glass shade, circa 1900. $3,375

Leaded glass and bronze miniature apple blossom lamp, by Tiffany, 18½in. high. $4,500

Tiffany Studio bronze table lamp, 34.5cm. high, 1910-20. $5,000

Acorn leaded glass table lamp by Tiffany Studios, New York, 23in. high. $5,210

Art Nouveau leaded glass and bronze table lamp, circa 1910, 64.5cm. high. $6,000

AMERICANA

TIFFANY LAMPS

Tiffany bronze and leaded glass table lamp, early 20th century, 24in. high. $6,500

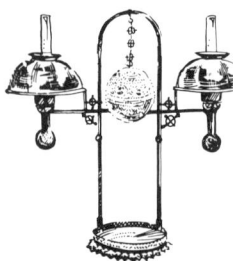

Early Favrile glass and silvered bronze kerosene student lamp, by Tiffany, 24in. high. $7,315

Early 20th century Tiffany bronze and Favrile glass ten-light lily table lamp, 20½in. high. $7,500

Turtle back leaded glass table lamp by Tiffany, 23½in. high. $7,500

Tiffany Studio bronze table lamp, circa 1900, 63cm. high. $8,100

Gilt bronze and glass linen gold table lamp by Tiffany, 24in. high. $8,500

Good Tiffany glass table lamp. $10,000

Tiffany bronze and leaded glass table lamp, 23in. high, New York, circa 1900. $10,000

Wild rose leaded glass and gilt bronze lamp by Tiffany, 22½in. high. $11,000

AMERICANA

TIFFANY LAMPS

L. C. Tiffany 'orange poppy' lampshade on Art Nouveau base, 50cm. diam. $11,000

Tiffany Studios daffodil lamp, marked on base, circa 1900, 66cm. high. $11,035

Daffodil leaded glass and gilt bronze table lamp by Tiffany Studios, New York. $12,720

Poppy leaded glass and gilt bronze table lamp, by Tiffany, 25½in. high. $14,625

Poppy leaded glass and bronze table lamp, by Tiffany, 27¼in. high. $24,750

Tiffany 'Mandarin' leaded glass shade and flowering lotus bronze table lamp base. $26,000

Tiffany Studio wisteria lamp. $47,250

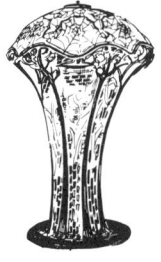

Spider web leaded glass, mosaic and bronze table lamp by Tiffany. $180,000

Tiffany spider web lamp with bronze baluster base. $185,625

AMERICANA

LANTERNS

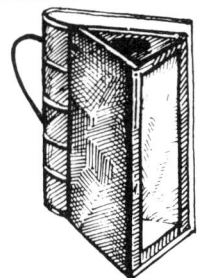

Early 19th century tin folding lantern in book form, 5½in. high. $100

Early 19th century tin and horn lantern, 15in. $150

Late 18th century brass traveling lantern with glass bull's eye door and tin top, 7½in. $150

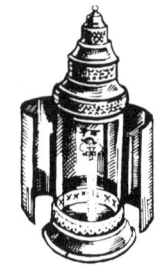

Early 19th century brass traveling lantern, sheet brass enclosing a glass cylinder, 7½in. $175

19th century wooden street lamp, with glass panels. $175

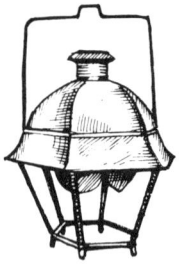

Early 19th century tin Argand-type outdoor lantern, hexagonal, 30in. $200

AMERICANA

LANTERNS

A late 18th century tin hand held lantern with a glazed door. $200

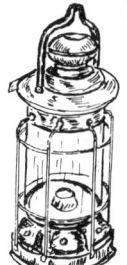

Early 19th century brass ship's mast lantern, 17¼in. high with glass cylinder. $275

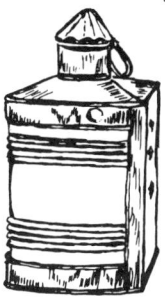

Mid 19th century ship's port lantern of copper and brass with ridged glass shade, 21½in. high. $300

18th century brass portable lantern with sliding brass door and hinged glass door, 6½in. high. $425

A fine quality 18th century tin lantern with glass panels, 18in. high. $500

Brass lantern with four glass panels and triple candleholder, 19in. $800

AMERICANA

MARBLE & STONE

19th century decorated marble pedestal, 8in. high. $50

19th century marble vase, 15in. high. $80

Marble bust of a young man, 55cm. high. $250

19th century white marble statuary bust of a girl, draped, 68cm. high. $300

Marble bust of Pharaoh's daughter, circa 1904, 26½in. high. $325

Large sculpture of a pouter pigeon, 1920's, 34.5cm. high, in composition stone. $655

American 20th century marble figure of a seated female nude, 53cm. high. $1,000

Late 19th century American marble bust of the Greek Slave, by H. Powers, 39.5cm. high. $6,185

Black marble sculpture modeled as a polished scorpion fish, signed, 15½in. high. $10,430

AMERICANA

MINIATURE FURNITURE

Miniature mahogany chest of drawers, circa 1850, 11½in. high. $195

Mid 19th century American miniature Empire grained pine bureau, 21in. high. $200

Mid 19th century American miniature Empire bureau, 9in. high. $275

American miniature walnut Renaissance revival bed, circa 1875, 21½in. long. $275

Mid 19th century American miniature Empire pine bureau, two drawers with maple veneer, 10¼in. high. $300

One of a pair of miniature corner chairs with bowed and carved crestings. $445

18th century American miniature pine painted desk with applied molding, 18½in. wide. $700

Mid 18th century miniature walnut bureau, 8½in. wide. $840

Miniature Chippendale maple and pine bureau, New England, circa 1780, 15in. wide. $2,200

AMERICANA

MIRRORS

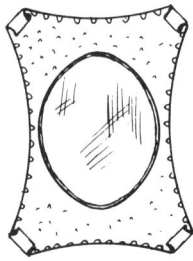

A small 20th century hammered pewter mirror 10in. high. $35

Early 20th century mahogany framed dressing mirror, 89cm. high. $50

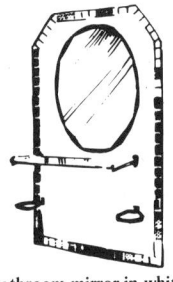

Bathroom mirror in white vitrolite, surrounded in pink mirror flex, 1940's. $100

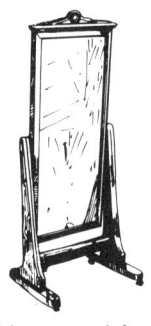

20th century oak framed cheval mirror. $150

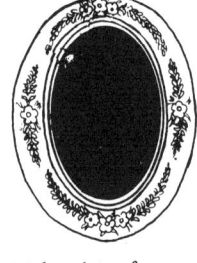

Cut glass picture frame by Hawkes, Corning, New York, circa 1900, 7in. long. $150

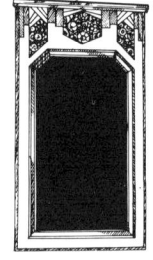

Large Art Deco mirror frame, early 1920's. $170

Early 19th century mahogany mirror stand, 20in. high. $170

An upright table mirror in Art Nouveau silver frame. $170

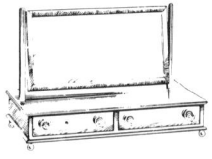

Early 19th century Federal shaving mirror, Portland, Maine, 17in. high. $225

AMERICANA

MIRRORS

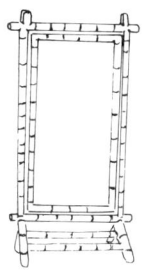

19th century ebonized and gilt bamboo pattern, framed cheval mirror. $250

19th century painted wood-encased mirror, 18in. wide. $250

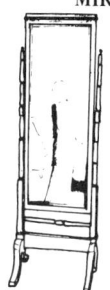

Early 20th century mahogany framed upright cheval mirror. $250

20th century American Chippendale style mahogany mirror with painted glass plates, 48in. high. $275

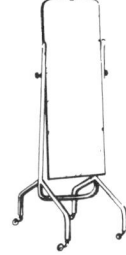

Chromed tubular steel cheval mirror on four castors, 1930's, 160cm. high. $300

One of a pair of silver, copper and wood Art Deco mirror frames, circa 1925, 62cm. high. $300

WMF silvered metal mirror frame, circa 1910, 40.75cm. high. $305

Hammered copper wall mirror, circa 1900, 76cm. wide. $350

Early 19th century American Federal mahogany shaving mirror with shield-shaped glass, 20in. wide. $350

AMERICANA

MIRRORS

Hammered pewter mirror with enamel blue decoration. $350

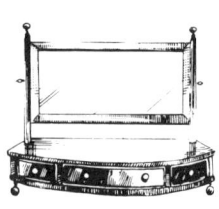

Early 19th century American mahogany shaving stand, drawers with turned ivory knobs, 19½in. wide. $425

A painted wood chinoiserie wall mirror, 1920's, 44½ x 18in. $450

Fine early Victorian cheval mirror. $450

Copper and enamel mirror, circa 1900, 40in. wide. $450

18th century American primitive wall mirror, with arched crest, 8 x 6in. $550

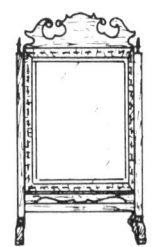

Late 18th century American transitional shaving mirror on stand, 11¼in. wide. $550

Mid 18th century American Queen Anne pine painted looking glass, 17in. high. $600

Late 19th century American Greco-Roman carved oak revival mirror. $650

AMERICANA

MIRRORS

Mahogany cheval mirror, 1850's, 78in. high. $750

New Hampshire mirror clock, circa 1820, by Benjamin Morrill, 32½in. high. $950

Art Nouveau bronze mirror case with the figure of a young woman, 31cm. high. $1,060

Chippendale mahogany veneer and gilt mirror, frame bordered with gilt applied decorations, circa 1760, 60in. high. $1,100

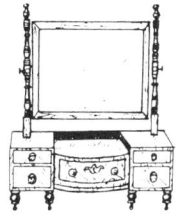

Federal mahogany and mahogany veneer shaving mirror on stand, circa 1800, 24½in. wide. $1,150

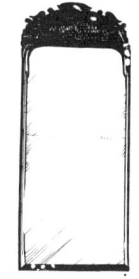

William and Mary mahogany mirror, circa 1730, with cut-out crest, 18in. wide. $1,350

Rococo revival walnut and burl walnut veneered dressing table, circa 1860, 60in. wide. $2,200

George II giltwood mirror, 75in. high. $5,000

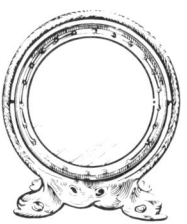

Tiffany Studios bronze and Favrile glass mirror, New York, circa 1920, 13in. high. $6,000

AMERICANA

MISCELLANEOUS

English/American wickerwork pram, 4ft.4in. long, 1930's. $70

One of a pair of early 19th century candlesticks, whale ivory and baleen overlay on hollywood, 9in. $110

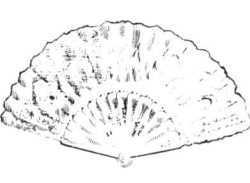

Tiffany & Co., fan with lace wing, veins of incised mother-of-pearl. $140

Early 19th century toleware tray, probably Connecticut, 12½in. long. $150

Standing figure of the Esso man, 5½in. high, on a radiator cap. $205

Late 19th century American pipe set in leather case. $220

Mickey Mouse glass car mascot, stamped Walt Disney Productions, circa 1940, 5¼in. high. $220

American decorated toleware tea tray, with rolled rim, circa 1850, 26in. wide. $300

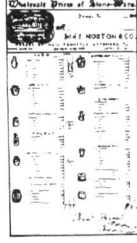

One of two 19th century framed stoneware price lists, Vermont, 13½in. high. $300

AMERICANA

MISCELLANEOUS

Toleware bread tray, probably New York, early 19th century, 13in. long. $370

20th century American Santa Claus hooked rug, 31¼ x 39in. $450

14kt. yellow gold and cut crystal flask by Tiffany & Co., 12.5cm. high. $800

Pair of late 19th century American walnut and stained glass doors, 27in. wide. $500

14kt. yellow gold mesh purse with engraved frame, cabochon garnet clasp and a pencil attached to one side. $800

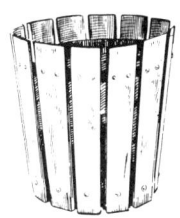

Gustav Stickley oak waste bucket, banded together with iron, 12in. diam. $950

Marilyn Monroe's pink-mesh bra. $1,000

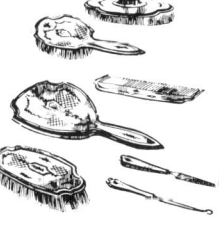

Early 20th century seven-piece 14 karat gold dresser set, Massachusetts. $2,000

Stovepipe bearskin hat belonging to Abraham Lincoln. $9,870

AMERICANA

MONEY BANKS

A late 19th century 'City Bank', 4½in. high. $70

An automated 'Jolly Nigger' money bank. $70

An original cast iron 'standing bear' money box, in two halves, secured from the back with a single screw, 6in. high. $80

An early 20th century cast alloy 'mule' money bank, 4¾in. long. $125

19th century American cast-iron mechanical bank 'Eagle & Eaglets'. $150

American cast-iron Tammany money bank, circa 1880. $200

Cast-iron 'Novelty Bank' money box with hinged front, 6½in. high, American, circa 1875. $215

Late 19th century American 'speaking dog' cast-iron money bank, 7¾in. long. $240

AMERICANA

MONEY BANKS

Late 19th century American cat and mouse money box, 8½in. high. $260

Late 19th century 'Trick Pony' cast iron money bank, 7½in. wide. $295

Late 19th century jockey and mule money box, 9¾in. long, by James H. Bowen. $305

Mickey Mouse tinplate mechanical bank, both sides having different scenes, circa 1930, 6¾in. high. $345

Late 19th century American Uncle Sam cast-iron mechanical bank by Shepard Hardware Co., 11½in. high. $285

Late 19th century American cast-iron negro and shack money bank, 4½in. long. $300

Late 19th century American cast-iron mechanical bank, 'Paddy and the Pig', 8in. high. $320

American late 19th century mechanical money box. $350

AMERICANA

MONEY BANKS

An American cast-iron mechanical money box in the shape of a kneeling Red Indian brave firing a gun at a brown bear. $360

An American cold-painted cast-iron 'Bucking Mule' money box, 8½in. long. $365

Late 19th century American owl cast-iron money bank, 7¾in. high. $385

A cold-painted cast-iron baseball money box, 9½in. wide. $385

A late 19th century American cold-painted cast-iron money box in the form of a soldier who fires a penny into a tree stump. $385

Late 19th century American cast-iron money bank, 10in. wide. $400

Late 19th century American 'Punch and Judy' money box, 7in. high. $400

American cast-iron mechanical money box in the form of a mule kicking over a Negro boy, the base bearing the title 'Always did 'spise a Mule'. $420

AMERICANA

MONEY BANKS

A cold-painted American cast-iron money box 'Always did 'spise a Mule', 10in. long. $430

Late 19th century American 'William Tell' mechanical shooting bank, 10¼in. long. $450

A U.S. iron money bank, depicting Jonah and the Whale, base 10in. long, stamped 'Pat. July 15, 1890'. $450

Late 19th century American cast-iron 'Punch and Judy' money box, 7½in. high. $450

Late 19th century cast-iron 'Organ Bank' money box, 4½in. high. $520

Late 19th century American 'Leap-Frog Bank', 7½in. wide. $620

Late 19th century American monkey and barrel-organ cast-iron money bank, 6½in. high. $620

Late 19th century American reclining Chinaman cast-iron mechanical bank, 8in. long. $1,035

AMERICANA

MUSICAL BOXES

Polyphon disk music box with serpentine front rosewood veneer case, 11in. wide. $550

Symphonion disk musical box in rosewood case, complete with twenty disks, 13¼in. long. $650

Symphonion disk musical box in maple case, with twenty-seven extra disks, 10¾in. wide. $750

Regina disk music box in cherry case with two disks, 14½in. wide. $900

Regina lift-top coin operated music box in carved oak case, sold with twenty disks, 21in. wide. $1,100

Criterion No. 5 disk music box in mahogany case, with matching stand, 26in. wide. $2,600

AMERICANA

MUSICAL BOXES

Regina music and gum machine in oak case with glass door, 16in. wide. $2,600

Sirion disk music box in inlaid fruit-wood case, complete with ten disks, 25in. wide. $3,250

Upright American symphonion in oak case, complete with ten disks, 28in. wide. $3,500

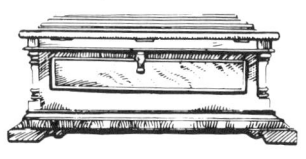

Regina accordion top disk music box in oak case, with thirteen disks, 34½in. wide. $4,500

Kalliope panorama automat disk music box in rosewood and walnut case, 25½in. wide. $5,000

Mira Orchestral Grand musical box, in mahogany case, 29½in. wide. $5,250

AMERICANA

ORGANS

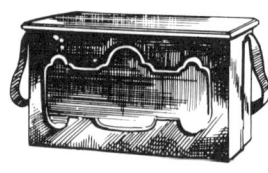

Small organ grinder in grain painted case, 12½in. wide. $170

Street automatic piano in beech case, slightly damaged, 40in. wide. $250

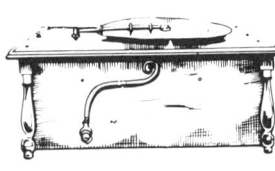

Amopette Atlas organette in black painted case, with twelve disks, 17in. wide. $275

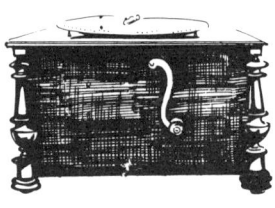

Amoretto disk organ in ebonized wood case with twelve disks, 20½in. wide. $500

Jazz band barrel organ in beech case, with automatic barrel, 32in. wide. $550

Early 20th century, 8¾in. chalet disk organette, 12in. wide, together with eighteen disks. $675

AMERICANA

ORGANS

Late 19th century American Celestina paper-roll organette, 38cm. wide. $875

Late 19th century American concert roller organ on oak case, 43cm. wide. $950

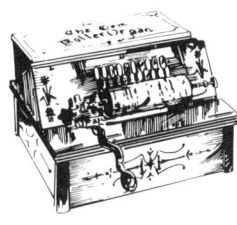

Gem roller organ in stencil-decorated wooden case, circa 1890, 36cm. wide. $950

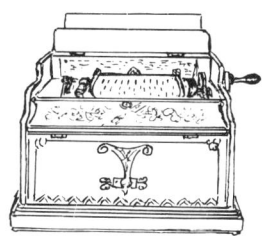

American Celestina paper-roll organette, circa 1880, 15in. wide. $1,000

Hurdy-Gurdy monkey organ in mahogany case, 18½in. wide. $2,300

Wurlitzer military band organ in oak case, 84in. wide, needs restored. $9,500

AMERICANA

PEWTER

Miniature ribbed pewter chamberstick, with bowl shaped drip pan, 2½in. $50

Early 19th century pewter half pint tankard in the shape of a tulip. $65

Late 18th century pewter canteen with decoration at throat and base, 27.5cm. high. $100

Mid 18th century pewter candlestick with baluster shaped stem, 6¾in. $110

WMF Art Nouveau wafer barrel and lid. $150

19th century pewter hot water jug with wood-mounted ribbed urn finial, 36cm. high. $300

Miniature pewter chamberstick, 2in. high. $350

WMF pewter mounted green glass decanter, circa 1900, 42cm. high. $390

Pewter pint mug by Thos. D. & Sherman Boardman, 1835, 4½in. high. $450

AMERICANA

PEWTER

WMF green glass and pewter claret jug of trumpet form, 40.5cm. high. $475

One of a pair of pewter whale oil lamps, New York, circa 1850, 10¼in. high. $475

'Flower' handle pewter porringer by Thomas D. & Sherman Boardman, circa 1820-30, 5¼in. diam. $525

WMF silvered pewter tazza, circa 1900, 21.5cm. high. $700

Large WMF pewter jardiniere, 32.5cm. wide, circa 1900. $745

One of a pair of painted pewter mantel ornaments, circa 1790, 12¼in. high. $750

One of a pair of early 18th century pewter pricket candlesticks with domed bases, 41cm. high. $800

WMF pewter candlestick, 26.25cm. high, circa 1900. $845

American pewter quart communion flagon by T. D. Boardman & Co., 1825-30, 8in. high. $1,150

AMERICANA

PHONOGRAPHS

Edison business phonograph, model D, American, circa 1908. $190

Edison home phonograph with black japanned shaped octagonal horn, patent date 1906. $205

An Edison Bell standard phonograph with loud speaker. $225

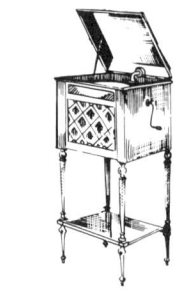

Edison diamond disk phonograph, circa 1915, in floor standing oak cabinet. $345

Columbia disk phonograph with outside horn, 78 speed, 10¾in. wide. $550

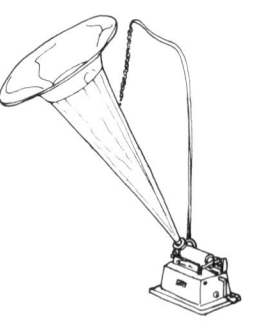

An Edison Gem phonograph, model C. $600

AMERICANA

PHONOGRAPHS

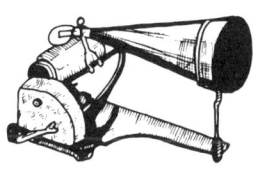

Columbia Puck type phonograph, model AQ, American, circa 1900. $625

Edison Gem phonograph, circa 1910. $650

Good Edison home phonograph, circa 1902, with 2ft.5½in. brass horn. $650

Edison home phonograph, circa 1901-1904, American, horn 27in. long. $650

Edison fireside phonograph, circa 1909, with approximately one hundred cylinders. $655

Edison standard phonograph, American, circa 1906-1908. $675

AMERICANA

PHONOGRAPHS

American Edison Gem phonograph, model D, with original crane, 1912, sold with cylinders. $760

American Edison home phonograph, 1906-1908. $800

Good Edison Amberola VIII phonograph, American, circa 1913. $1,000

Edison Gem phonograph with two and four minute gearing, American, 1905-1908. $1,000

Edison Bell Gem phonograph model A, American, 1908-1912. $1,000

Edison fireside phonograph, circa 1910. $1,000

AMERICANA

PHONOGRAPHS

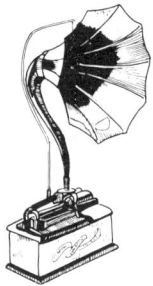

Edison home phonograph in a light oak case, American, circa 1904. $1,250

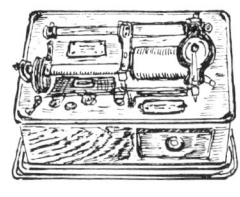

Edison spring motor phonograph, American, circa 1898-1901. $1,500

Fine diamond disk phonograph in Chippendale style cabinet, American, circa 1925. $1,750

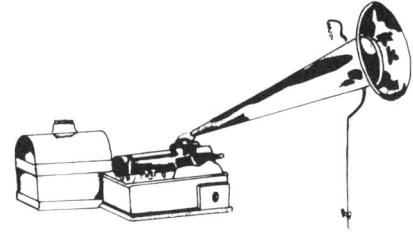

Good and rare Edison spring motor phonograph in oak cabinet, American, circa 1896-1900. $2,500

Edison opera phonograph, No 2948, with self-supporting laminated horn, circa 1912. $3,740

Edison home phonograph with Bettini attachment. $4,000

AMERICANA

PIANOS

19th century rosewood framed upright pianoforte with brass candle sconces. $300

Steinway & Sons ebonized wood upright piano, New York, circa 1903, 62in. wide. $300

Haines Bros. player piano with ampico action, complete with thirty-six rolls, 63in. wide. $700

Fine 19th century boudoir upright pianoforte in satinwood with marquetry inlay, 4ft.7in. $1,310

A large and ornate upright piano by Steinway & Sons, New York, each surface with carved and gilt scrolls on a green ground, 5ft.4in. wide. $2,000

Arts & Crafts oak piano by Vose & Sons, Boston, Massachusetts, circa 1910, 60½in. wide. $3,400

AMERICANA

PICTURES

Late 18th century silk embroidered floral group. $100

19th century woolwork picture of a sailing ship. $300

Early film poster for Keystone Comedies, framed and glazed, 43in. high. $355

Early 19th century American embroidered picture on a silk ground, 15 x 18½in. $400

One of a pair of American framed needlework pictures, 1721, 10 x 10½in. $900

Rare late 18th century feather picture, 28 x 33in. $3,500

AMERICANA

QUILTS

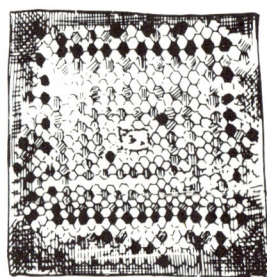

Chintz patchwork bedcover with square central medallion and broad border, 65 x 60in. $145

Mid 19th century dated applique coverlet of white cotton squares with leaf patterns, 84in. wide. $175

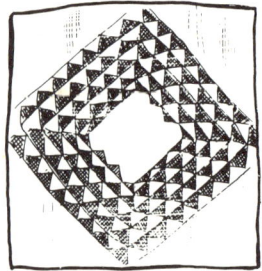

Late 19th/early 20th century American patchwork quilt in navy blue and white triangles, 75½in. square. $300

Late 19th century patchwork quilt of flying geese design on a gray calico ground. $300

20th century tapework bedcover with central flower, 113in. square. $305

Mid 19th century American quilted patchwork coverlet, 72 x 90in. $325

QUILTS

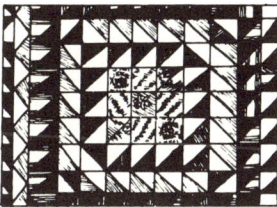

Silk patchwork bedcover lined with Paisley pattern cotton, circa 1830, 89in. square. $335

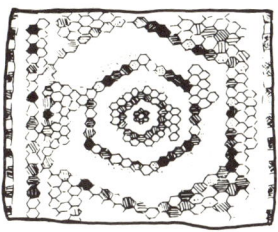

Early 19th century patchwork quilt in hexagonal, square and triangles, 94 x 87in. $345

Patchwork quilt with central flower medallion, circa 1820, 108in. square. $345

White American Marseilles-type quilt with cotton face, circa 1820, 80 x 66in. $350

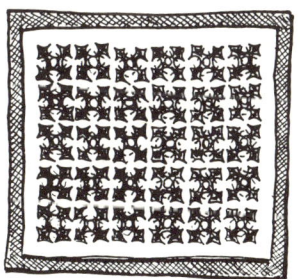

Late 19th century American appliqued friendship quilt, 85in. square. $350

19th century appliqued quilt, Rhode Island, on cotton print background. $350

AMERICANA

QUILTS

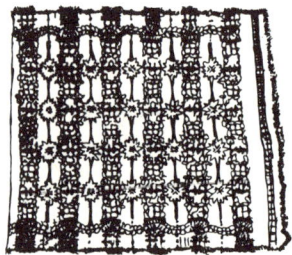

Mid 19th century American jacquard coverlet in wool on cotton ground, 88 x 78in. $375

Late 19th century bedcover made from officer's uniforms, 91½ x 77in. $395

Bethlehem star appliqued and pierced quilt, circa 1925. $400

19th century American appliqued and patchwork quilt, 88 x 94in. $400

Late 19th century embroidered bedspread on a midnight-blue satin ground, 99 x 85in. $430

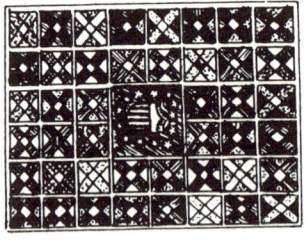

Civil War patriotic quilt, 66 x 88in., dated 1864. $450

AMERICANA

QUILTS

19th century pieced and appliqued quilt, slightly faded, 84in. square. $450

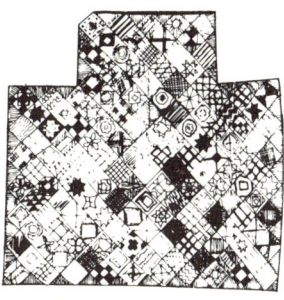

Antique Baltimore friendship quilt, dated 1843, 108in. wide. $450

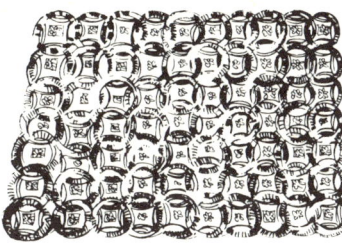

American patchwork quilt in pastel colors, circa 1875. $500

19th century American pieced appliqued quilt with white cotton field, 102 x 82in. $600

Late 18th century quilted calamanco and wool patchwork coverlet, American, 92in. square. $600

Striking patchwork quilt of tiny hexagons using late 18th/early 19th century chintzes. $660

AMERICANA

QUILTS

Mid 19th century flowerpot and grapevine appliqued quilt, Pennsylvania, 80in. square. $675

Embroidered silk bedcover with pheasant on a tree, circa 1900, 92 x 74½in. $695

Pennsylvania pieced quilt of 'Spider's Web' pattern in multi-colored cottons, 84in. square, 1860-70. $730

Early 18th century embroidered bedcover sold with three pillow-cases with white cotton ground. $770

Applique coverlet, Pennsylvania, circa 1860, 84in. square. $800

Mid 18th century embroidered cotton bedcover with white ground and green threads, 92 x 85in. $850

AMERICANA

QUILTS

Late 19th century American Victorian crazy quilt with matching shams, 76in. square. $1,000

Mid 18th century American crewelwork coverlet on handwoven cotton sheeting, 94 x 98in. $1,200

American patriotic coverlet in cotton sewn to give the effect of the American flag, 7ft.6in. square, circa 1880. $1,200

Early 19th century embroidered satin bedcover with central medallion, 91½ x 84in. $1,540

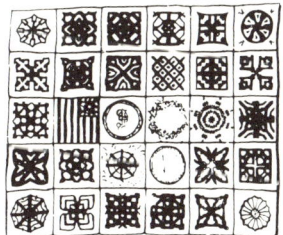

Applique commemorative coverlet of thirty quilted squares, 1853, 93in. square. $2,700

Brocade bedcover of gold thread on crimson ground, circa 1900, 102 x 71¾in. $3,150

SAMPLERS

18th century needlework sampler by Mary Adamson, 1781, 31cm. high. $150

Early 19th century needlework sampler by Selina Doughty, 1835, framed and glazed, 38 x 32cm. $260

Sampler worked with a house and a verse by Maria Norman, 1832, 16 x 12in. $265

Late 18th century needlework sampler, altered, framed and glazed, 31.5cm. square. $335

American needlework sampler with wide floral border, circa 1825, 18in. square. $350

Child's sampler in good condition, 1819. $365

SAMPLERS

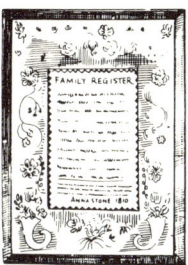

'Stone' family register by Anna Stone, 1810, 21½ x 15½in. $400

Needlework family record by Martha A Chamberlain, Westmoreland, New Hampshire, 1833, 17 x 21in. $550

Dean family needlework memorial, circa 1800, Massachusetts, 17¼ x 16in. $1,000

Needlework sampler in circular reserve on linen ground, 1817, 20½ x 19½in. $1,300

One of two frame needlework samplers, American, 19th century. $2,200

Needlework sampler by Sally Oliver, 1801, of Upper Beverley, America, 19½ x 21in. $5,500

AMERICANA

SCRIMSHAW

19th century scrimshaw cow horn, circa 1840, 8½in. long. $170

Mid 19th century American pair of whale's tooth scrimshaw, mounted on wooden plinths, 14.5cm. high. $240

Late 19th century malacca walking cane with scrimshaw ball grip set with a compass, 81.5cm. long. $245

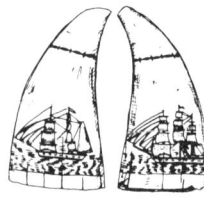

Late 19th century pair of whale's tooth scrimshaw, 11.5cm. high. $290

19th century engraved scrimshaw whale's tooth, 7in. high. $300

Early scrimshaw dipper, 18in. long. $450

Whale tooth engraved with a sailing ship at anchor and a sailor with his concubine, initialed by J. A., 4 x 2in. $475

Late 19th century pair of whale's tooth scrimshaw, one entitled 'Jane' the other 'Eliza', 12cm. high. $485

Early 19th century American scrimshaw jagging wheel in the form of a horse's head, 6in. long. $550

AMERICANA

SCRIMSHAW

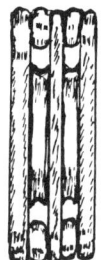

Rare, large scrimshaw working double block, 5¾in. wide. $620

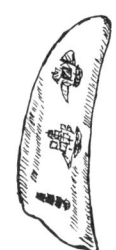

Early scrimshaw whale's tooth, 6in. long. $700

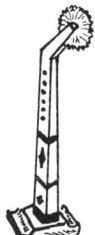

Very fine jagging wheel, 6½in. long. $750

Rare scrimshaw coatrack, 23¾in. long. $1,070

A whale's tooth color engraved to depict on one side a three-master lying offshore, and on the other a harbor scene, 8in. long. $1,000

Large scrimshaw swift, 23½in. high. $865

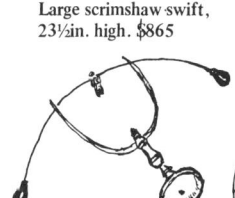

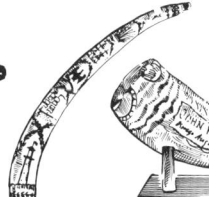

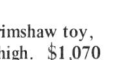

Rare scrimshaw toy, 12½in. high. $1,070

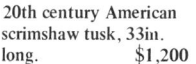

20th century American scrimshaw tusk, 33in. long. $1,200

Mid 18th century engraved powder horn, New York, 13in. long. $1,850

AMERICANA

SCREENS

19th century lithophane screen on turned baluster stem, with Madonna and Child. $100

Early 20th century painted three-fold screen in mahogany frames, 71in. high. $205

Late 19th century American stained glass firescreen with brass frame, 24in. wide. $425

Mid 19th century oak firescreen with numerous bevel-glazed panels. $550

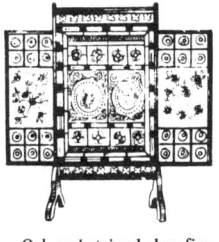

Oak and stained glass firescreen with two leaded glass doors, circa 1870, 112cm. wide. $740

Giltwood and stained glass screen, circa 1900, 62in. wide. $1,015

Mid 18th century Queen Anne mahogany pole screen, 56in. high. $2,500

American leaded glass firescreen, circa 1900, 45¼in. high. $3,825

Chippendale carved mahogany pole screen, 4ft. 10½in. high. $10,000

AMERICANA

SIGNS

18th century painted tin trade sign with decanter set in a laurel wreath. $250

American locksmith's sign in the form of a carved wooden key, circa 1900, 76in. long. $300

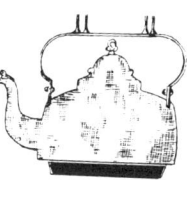

American kettle advertising sign in metal with iron handle, 22½in. high. $500

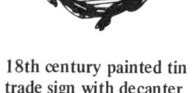

American bicycle shop sign, circa 1900, with applied molding, 77in. wide. $600

18th century tobacconist's sign of Red Indian figure. $985

Antique carved walnut tobacconist's sign modeled as a rotund Turk, 22in. high. $1,200

19th century American molded copper fish sign, gold leafed, 36in. long. $1,350

Early 19th century carved wooden mermaid Tavern sign, 55cm. long. $1,500

Hodges Inn sign with oval shield, Vermont, circa 1790, 31¾in. wide. $5,000

AMERICANA

SILVER BOWLS

20th century sterling silver handled bowl of oval form, 15¼in. long, 37.8 Troy oz. $325

Sterling silver fruit bowl, Connecticut, early 20th century, 4½in. high, 46 Troy oz. $450

Late 19th century Tiffany & Co. standing fruit bowl, New York, 10¼in. diam., 28 Troy oz. $600

Jensen silver bowl and spoon, 10cm. high, circa 1947. $645

An American circular bowl, 5¼in. high, circa 1800, 10oz.14dwt. $1,080

Late 18th century Central American circular bowl and cover, 16cm. diam., 680gr. $1,515

Gorham sterling silver punch bowl with lion mask and loose ring handles, 25cm. high, 78oz. $2,000

United States sterling silver punch bowl with matching ladle and three of the twelve cups, 189oz. $4,870

Rare early American silver punch bowl by John Coney. $45,000

AMERICANA

SILVER CANDLESTICKS

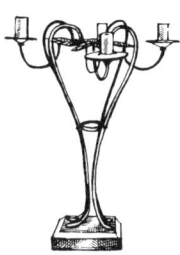

Late 18th century silver plated candelabrum with cast applied leaf decoration, 5in. high. $50

One of a pair of chromed metal candlesticks, 1930's, 55.75cm. high. $265

One of a pair of WMF electroplated candlesticks, circa 1900, 27cm. high. $430

One of a pair of early 19th century three-light plated candelabra, 45cm. high. $450

One of a pair of silver plated three-light candelabra, 56cm. high. $950

One of a pair of Georg Jensen silver candlesticks, circa 1920, 5½in. high. $2,250

One of a pair of 20th century Georg Jensen silver candelabra, 8½in. high, 70 Troy oz. $3,700

One of a pair of early 18th century table candlesticks by Blas Antonio de la Cruz, 13cm. high. $3,785

One of a pair of WMF silvered metal candelabra, circa 1900, 50.5cm. high. $3,925

AMERICANA

SILVER CENTERPIECES

Unusual late 19th century sterling silver and cut glass flower center, 7¼in. high, Eastern United States. $300

Sterling silver centerpiece by Bailey, Banks & Biddle, 37.5cm. diam., 41oz. $975

Georg Jensen silver centerpiece, 10¼in. diam. $1,855

COMPOTES

Sterling silver compote by Duhme Co., Ohio, circa 1900, 9½in. high, 18 Troy oz. $150

Early 20th century American sterling silver compote by S. Kirk, 25cm. diam., 19oz. $250

One of a pair of Tiffany & Co., enameled silver comports, 14cm. high, 22oz. $610

Georg Jensen silver compote, 20th century, 9½in. diam., 28 Troy oz. $1,000

Silver compote by S. Kirk & Son, with removable rim and embossed decoration, 42oz. $1,100

Large Jensen coupe with bell-shaped bowl, 1936, 19cm. high. $1,405

AMERICANA

SILVER CUPS

Sterling silver and agate three-handled loving cup, circa 1900, 4½in. diam. $200

Gorham sterling silver chalice in Renaissance revival style, Rhode Island, circa 1864, 9½in. high, 14½ Troy oz. $275

American silver cylinder-shaped mug by R. & W. Wilson, circa 1835, 7oz. 10dwt., 10cm. high. $350

Fireman's coin silver chalice by John Curry, Philadelphia, 17½ Troy oz., 9½in. high. $400

Silver presentation cup, body heavily embossed, sold by Black, Starr & Frost, New York, 1876, 9in. high, 17 Troy oz. $550

Martele sterling silver loving cup, Rhode Island, circa 1920, 30 Troy oz., 7¾in. high. $1,100

Early 20th century sterling silver cup, Towle Silversmiths, Massachusetts, 18in. high, 215.6 Troy oz. $1,950

Footed silver cann by Samuel Bartlett, Boston, circa 1790, 14 Troy oz., 5¾in. high. $2,300

American silver cann with molded lip and pedestal foot, 5½in. high, 14 Troy oz. $4,915

AMERICANA

SILVER DISHES

Small Jensen silver footed dish, 5.25cm. high, 1936. $395

Arts & Crafts hammered copper and silver chafing dish, American, circa 1910, 20½in. long. $450

WMF silvered metal Art Nouveau dish, 47cm. wide, circa 1900. $450

Sterling silver fruit basket with cast handle, 13½in. wide. $525

18th century South American shaving dish, 17½in. wide, circa 1760, 38oz. 5dwt. $700

Large silvered metal Art Nouveau centerpiece, circa 1900, 45cm. high. $740

American silver porringer by Edward Winslow, Boston, circa early 18th century, 12cm. diam. $800

WMF silvered metal dish, 21cm. high, circa 1900. $810

AMERICANA

SILVER DISHES

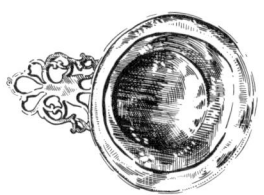

Mid 18th century silver porringer by J. Hurd, Boston, 5in. diam. $850

Late 18th century American silver porringer with dome bottom and pierced handle, 5¼in. diam. $950

Large South American sideboard dish, 16¾in. diam., 18th century, 62oz. 12dwt. $1,215

Plain silver brandy saucepan, by John Le Roux, New York, circa 1740, 14oz. 7dwt. $1,620

Central American ecuelle and cover, Guatemala, circa 1760, 18.2cm. diam., 845gr. $1,890

Gorham sterling silver dish with overturned lip, 45cm. long, 110oz.8dwt. $2,600

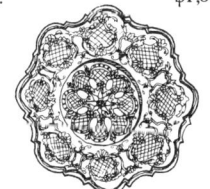

Mid 18th century Central American dish, by Gueixa, Guatemala, 36cm. diam., 19oz.6dwt. $2,975

American silver porringer by Paul Revere Snr., engraved handle, 19cm. long. $3,900

AMERICANA

SILVER FLATWARE

Georg Jensen silver serving spoon and fork, circa 1920. $370

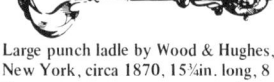

Large punch ladle by Wood & Hughes, New York, circa 1870, 15¼in. long, 8 Troy oz. $475

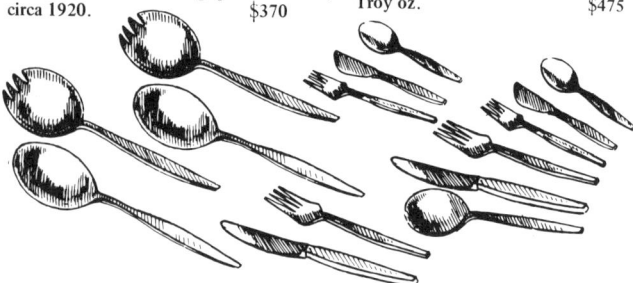

Part of a seventy-eight piece Georg Jensen silver flatware service in the Cypress pattern, 1954. $1,970

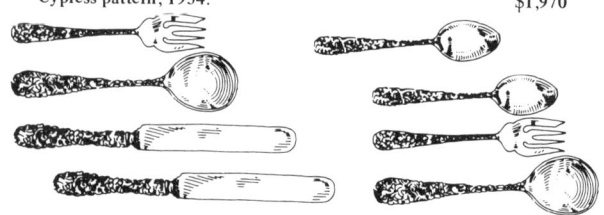

Part of a large lot of early 20th century American flower pattern tableware, mostly silver, by Stieff Co., Baltimore. $3,375

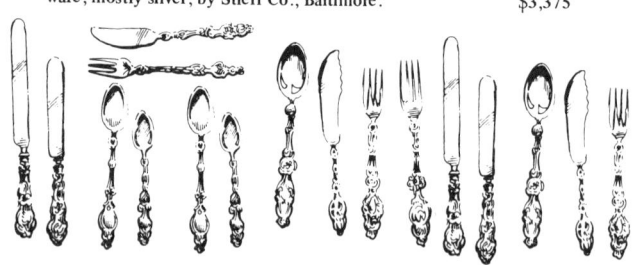

Part of a large set of sterling silver flatware by Whiting Manufacturing Co., Rhode Island, early 20th century. $4,900

AMERICANA

SILVER FLATWARE

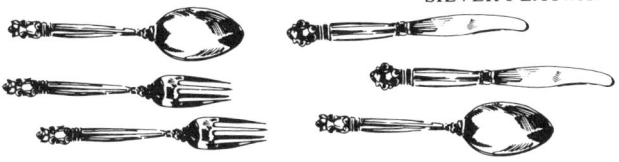

Part of a large set of Jensen tableware, 1930's, 4.407gm. $5,150

Part of a Georg Jensen table service of eighty-four pieces, 1939, 106oz.
$5,305

Part of a Georg Jensen silver flatware service in cactus pattern, ninety-four pieces. $5,400

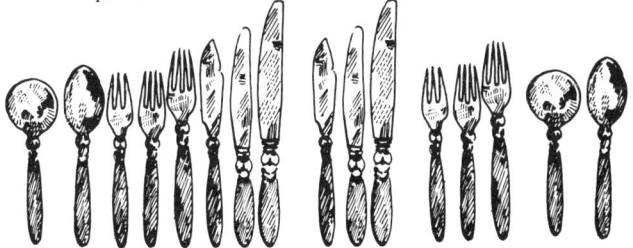

Part of a ninety-six piece Jensen service in silver colored metal. $5,615

AMERICANA

SILVER JUGS

Tiffany silver sauceboat, New York, circa 1860, with scrolled handle, 9 Troy oz., 6in. high. $200

Mid 19th century silver water pitcher with shaped rim and pouring spout, 11in. high, 23 Troy oz. $250

20th century American silver presentation ewer of helmet shape, 14in. high, 32 Troy oz. $300

Victorian silver plated Renaissance style ewer, 42.5cm. high. $425

Regency style silver hot water jug, 1898, 25oz., 9in. high. $480

Gorham sterling silver pitcher in Renaissance revival style, Rhode Island, circa 1864, 15½in. high. $500

American presentation silver water pitcher by B. Gardiner, New York, circa 1830, 26oz.14dwt., 31cm. high. $500

Silver coffee pot by Georg Jensen, 1925, 7¾in. high, 19oz. $510

Sterling silver coffee pot by R. & W. Wilson, Philadelphia, 22oz.18dwt., 29cm. high. $525

AMERICANA

SILVER JUGS

Late 19th century Gorham sterling silver water pitcher, 10¼in. high, 40 Troy oz. $625

American silver flask-shaped wine ewer and tray by Gorham Mfg. Co., Providence, R.I., 1882, 1,027gm. $850

American silver ewer by J. & I. Cox, New York, circa 1835, 34oz.10dwt., 12¼in. high. $965

Jensen silver jug, designed by Johan Rohde, 1920, 22.75cm. high. $1,045

Victorian rococo revival coin silver water pitcher by Jones Ball & Poor, Boston, circa 1852, 33 Troy oz., 11in. high. $1,100

Jensen silver jug, 1926, 16.5cm. high. $1,150

American silver footed cream jug with high pouring spout by John Allen, Boston, 3in. high, 3 Troy oz. $1,700

Early 19th century silver wine ewer. $2,000

American silver tankard by Benjamin Burt, Boston, circa 1770, 26oz.8dwt., 22.5cm. high. $4,000

AMERICANA

MISCELLANEOUS SILVER

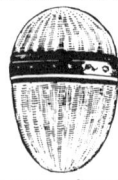

20th century sterling silver and enamel thimble case of egg shape, 4cm. high. $185

Jensen silver cruet, circa 1950-55. $305

One of a pair of late 19th century silver peacocks, 14oz., 27.5cm. long. $350

American Kutani and sterling silver inkstand, circa 1900, 12¼in. long, by John Wanamaker. $550

17th century silver box, 16.5cm. wide. $650

Silver caster by Zachariah Bridgden, Boston, Massachusetts, 1734-87, 5¾in. high, 4 Troy oz. $750

Jensen cocktail shaker designed by Harold Nielsen, in three sections, 28cm. high, 1930's. $1,400

Late 18th century South American casket with domed hinged cover, 22cm. wide, 1325gm. $2,460

AMERICANA

SILVER TEAPOTS

19th century plated teapot with ivory handle. $50

19th century plated teapot with ebony handle and finial. $55

Victorian silver teapot by Squire & Brother Co., New York, circa 1850, 19.5 Troy oz., 7in. high. $275

Tiffany sterling silver and copper teapot, circa 1890, 12.5cm. high. $600

American coin silver teapot by Shepherd & Boyd, Albany, circa 1815, 36oz.16dwt., 25cm. high. $650

Coin silver footed teapot by C. Bard & Son, Pennsylvania, circa 1850, 36oz., 27.5cm. high. $850

American silver teapot by Steven Burdet, New York, circa 1730, 15oz., 12.7cm. high. $5,500

13th century American teapot, 4¾in. high, porbably by William Pollard of Boston, circa 1730, 15oz.5dwt. $10,000

AMERICANA

SILVER TEASETS

Unusual three-piece electroplated coffee service, 1930's. $205

A silvered teaset of the 1930's. $450

Four-piece electroplated tea and coffee set and a matching tea kettle, stand and burner, circa 1860. $515

AMERICANA

SILVER TEASETS

Late 19th century Art Nouveau silver teaset of three pieces. $715

Six-piece sterling silver teaset by Shreve, Crump & Low Co., Boston, circa 1875, 118½ troy oz. $1,200

Gorham sterling silver teaset, Rhode Island, 1960, 60 troy oz. $1,250

AMERICANA

SILVER TEASETS

American three-piece teaset with faceted bodies, circa 1830, by N.J. Bogert, 74.1oz. $1,390

Mid 20th century four-piece tea and coffee service by Birks, Canada, 99.9oz. $1,730

Five-piece silver tea service in Egyptian style by Gorham, 90 Troy oz. $2,000

AMERICANA

SILVER TEASETS

Late 18th century New York silver three-piece teaset by Joel Sayre, 45oz.
$2,500

Seven-piece tea and coffee set with two-handled tray, by Tiffany & Co., 239oz. $3,235

Georg Jensen teaset and tray, fully London import marked. $3,645

AMERICANA

SILVER TEASETS

Jensen four-piece coffee set, circa 1930. $3,715

Gorham repousse sterling silver teaset, Rhode Island, circa 1891, 116 Troy oz. $4,200

Reed & Barton sterling silver teaset, Chippendale style, 186 Troy oz. $4,200

AMERICANA

SILVER TEASETS

Four-piece Jensen silver tea service with ivory side handles, circa 1926-29.
$4,445

Seven-piece sterling silver tea and coffee service, New York, circa 1890, 297 Troy oz. $8,400

Six-piece tea and coffee service by Rand W. Wilson, Philadelphia, circa 1825. $8,815

AMERICANA

SILVER TRAYS

American Gorham sterling silver tray with beaded rim, 46oz., 47cm. long, circa 1898. $225

18th century George II sterling silver footed salver, 21oz., 23cm. diam. $900

Early 19th century American silver salver by John W. Forbes, New York, circa 1815, 11¾in. wide, 24oz.14dwt. $1,250

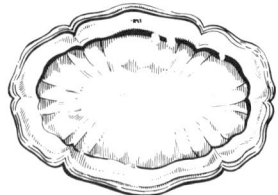

Central American oval silver basin, late 18th century, 985gr., 36.1cm. wide. $1,610

SILVER TUREENS

Lobed oval two-handled soup tureen and cover by Gorham Manufacturing Co., America, 36.7oz., circa 1910, 32cm. wide. $620

Floral repousse sterling silver soup tureen by S. Kirk & Son, 72oz.14dwt., 64cm. long. $2,500

Large Gorham sterling silver tureen. $3,240

One of a pair of Gorham sterling silver tureens. $4,105

AMERICANA

SILVER VASES

One of a pair of silver bottle vases, circa 1890. $105

Sterling silver vase by Arthur Stone, Gardner, Massachusetts, circa 1920's, 10 Troy oz., 6¾in. high. $120

Art Nouveau double-handled flower vase, 8¾in. high. $180

Art Nouveau large circular double-handled silver flower vase, 12in. high, 18oz.10dwt. $180

Art Nouveau silver flower vase with pierced and chased flowers, 9¾in. high, 8oz. $225

Large Art Deco electroplated vase, urn-shaped on pedestal foot, 1920's, 47cm. high. $285

Art Nouveau sterling silver vase by Goff, Washbourne & Dunn, New York, circa 1900, 20 Troy oz., 13in. high. $325

Georg Jensen trumpet-shaped silver vase, 1929, 15.5cm. high, 6¾oz. $510

WMF silver metal vase with twin whiplash handles, 23.5cm. high, circa 1900. $770

AMERICANA

TOYS

One from a set of eight Britain's United States Aviation men in peaked caps. $70

Early 20th century toy vehicles in excellent condition, 18¾in. and 23½in. wide. $80

American Louis Marx design tin-plate toy, 'Goofy Gardener'. $120

Mid 19th century American dancing negress toy, 7¾in. long, with key. $130

Stuffed toy 'Minnie Mouse' by Dean's Rag Book Ltd., circa 1930, 7in. high. $135

Mid 19th century rooster in felt and rabbit hair, 6in. high. $150

Marx tin wind-up 'Tidy Tim', New York, 1933, in excellent condition, 9in. long. $160

One of six tin wind-up toys, circa 1925-50, 3¾in. to 8¾in. high. $190

AMERICANA

TOYS

Wolverine 'Sunny Andy Kiddie Kampers', Pittsburgh, 1928, 14in. long. $190

Two Fun-e-Flex painted wooden toys, Mickey and Minnie Mouse, circa 1931, American, 6¾in. high. $205

Early 20th century American wicker baby carriage with parasol, 56½in. high. $225

Ham and Sam 'The Minstrel Team', by Ferdinand Strauss Corporation, New York, 1921, 7½in. high. $230

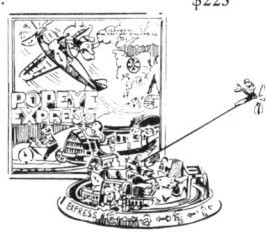

Marx lithographed tin wind-up 'Popeye Express', New York, 1935, in original box, 9in. diam. $250

Papier mache figure of 'Nipper', the R.C.A. trademark, 17½in. high. $300

Late 19th century mechanical duck in felt-covered papier mache, 12in. high. $325

Marx lithographed tin wind-up 'Donald Duck Duet', New York, 1946, in good condition, 9in. high. $325

AMERICANA

TOYS

American Zilotone tinplate musical toy, by Wolverine Supply & Manufacturing Co., 19cm. wide. $335

American child's pedal car, circa 1925, by Steelcraft, 36in. long. $350

Late 19th century American rocking horse with horsehair mane and tail, 47in. long. $400

Automaton magician, 52½in. high, 36½in. wide. $450

'Buddy L Model T' pickup truck, East Moline, Illinois, circa 1925, 12in. long. $525

American carved and painted stagecoach model and four-horse team, circa 1900, 53in. long. $550

Spic and Span 'The Hams What Am', by Louis Marx & Co., New York, circa 1925, 10in. high. $575

Early 20th century Steiff ride-on donkey and two-wheel cart, 47in. long. $575

AMERICANA

TOYS

Schoenhut 'Barney Goggle' and 'Spark Plug', Pennsylvania, circa 1924, 6in. and 7in. high. $675

Cast iron 'Old Dutch' pull toy, America, circa 1925, 9in. long. $725

American carved wood and painted carousel horse on fitted base, 47in. high. $1,000

Stevens & Brown tin mechanical Champion velocipede, patented 1870, 9¼in. high. $1,000

American Victorian pennyfarthing bicycle, circa 1880, 5ft. high. $1,000

Early American tinplate Mickey Mouse clockwork toy, circa 1930. $1,080

Early American hand-enameled tinplate horse and carriage, circa 1880, 15½in. long. $1,105

Hubley two-seated brake drawn by a pair of horses, 16½in. long. $4,000

AMERICANA

WEATHERVANES

Copper running horse weathervane with hollow body, 23½in. high. $475

American molded metal Gabriel weathervane, 31½in., circa 1870. $500

Late 19th century American gilded stagecoach weathervane on modern tripod base, 34½in. long. $500

A metal weathervane of a flying griffon, the Roman capital letters in thick copper, circa 1810. $585

19th century copper eagle weathervane, from Massachusetts, 30in. long. $600

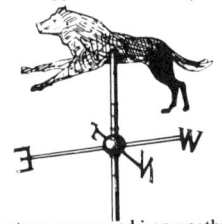

18th century copper and iron weathervane, 65in. high overall. $630

20th century wrought iron and copper pea fowl weathervane, American, 30½in. wide. $700

Rare 17th century copper weathervane in the shape of the 'Mayflower'. $700

AMERICANA

WEATHERVANES

Mid 19th century running horse weathervane, Boston Massachusetts, 27½in. wide. $700

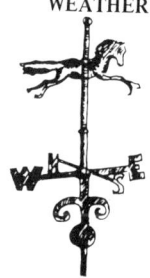

Cast metal horse weathervane, 39in. high, circa 1830. $745

A good copper, brass and wrought iron weathercock, 40in. high. $935

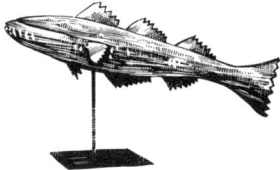

Late 19th century wooden fish weathervane, Massachusetts, 31in. long. $1,050

Late 19th century sheet metal butterfly weathervane, American, in copper. $1,100

Late 19th century American cast iron rooster weathervane, 23½in. long. $1,100

Mid 19th century American metal rooster weathervane, 24in. high. $1,500

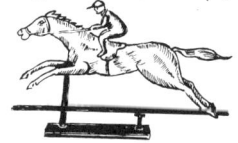

American copper horse and rider weathervane, circa 1900, 31in. long. $1,500

AMERICANA

INDEX

Adamson, Mary 218
Albany 235
Albertine 155
Allen, John 233
Altizimuth 166
Always Did 'Spise A Mule 198, 199
Amberina 157, 173
American Typewriter Co. 167
American Watch Co. 47
Amopette 202
Amusement Machines 14, 15
Andirons 21, 49, 168
Ansonia 42, 44
Ansonia Clock Co. 42
Appeal Of The Great Spirit 21
Argand 30, 186
Armchairs 58-63
Arts & Crafts 54, 55, 58, 62, 64, 210, 228
A.S.F. 33
Athapaskan 8, 9
Aurene 157

Baby Carriage 245
Bailey, Banks & Biddle 226
Baird, Edward P. 45
Bal-Ami 172
Baltimore 74, 215, 230
Bard, C. 235
Barney Goggle 247
Barnum, P. J. 26
Barometer 167
Barrel Bitters 142
Bartlett, Samuel 227
Beau Brummel 132

Beds 52, 53
Belter, John Henry 107
Bethlehem 214
Bettini 209
Bidet 112
Bininger, A. M. 142
Birks 238
Black Boy 43
Black, Starr & Frost 227
Blackamoor 28
Blackfoot 9
Blanket Box 74, 75
Blanket Chest 80
Boardman 204, 205
Bogert, N. J. 238
Bonnet 8, 10
Bookcases 54
Bookends 20
Bookstand 113
Boston 34, 36, 43, 47, 47, 58, 62, 130, 141, 155, 169, 210, 227, 228, 233-235, 237, 249
Bottles 142, 143
Bowen, James H. 197
Bowls, Glass 144-147
Bowls, Silver 224
Boxes 16-19
Bradley & Hubbard 43, 174
Brass 48-49
Breastplate 10
Bridgden, Zachariah 234
Brighton 33
Bristol 45
Bronze 20-23
Brookline 102
Brooks, T. 114
Bucking Mule 198
Buckley & Co. 14

Bull, John 43
Burden Strap 12
Burdet, Steven 235
Burt, Benjamin 233
Burton, H. 20
Butlers Desk 89
Butter Marker 24-27
Butterfly Table 134, 135

Cabinets 55
Caines, Thomas 153
Caldwell, J. E. 39
Camerden & Foster 38
Candelabrum 22, 23
Candle Box 16-18
Candle Holder 168, 169
Candle Mold 168
Candlestands 56, 57
Candlesticks 20-23, 48, 49, 148, 149, 155, 194, 204, 205, 225
Cann 227
Canterbury 112, 114, 115
Cape Fox 13
Card Tables 128-130
Carousel Horse 28, 29
Carter, L. F. & W. W. 45
Carved Wood 24-29
Castor Set 154
Celestina 203
Cellaret 19
Centerpieces 226, 228
Chairs 58-73
Chalkware 35, 36
Chamberlain, Martha 219
Chamberstick 24, 204
Champion 247
Chandeliers 30, 31
Chantel 172

250

AMERICANA

Chests 74, 75
Chests on Chests 82
Chests of Drawers 76-81
China 32-37
China Cabinets 83
Chippendale 40, 41, 53-57, 69, 70, 76-82, 84, 86, 87, 90-94, 96, 98, 100, 102, 103, 105-107, 123, 130-134, 139, 140, 189, 191, 193, 209, 222, 240
Cincinnati 32, 34, 36, 37, 88
City Bank 196
Civil War 17, 214
Cloak 13
Clock Sets 38, 39
Clocks 38-46
Club 11, 12
Clum, H. A. 167
Coat Rack 115, 221
Cocktail Cabinet 55
Cocktail Shaker 234
Coca Cola 166
Coconut Shell 24
Columbia 164, 167, 206, 207
Commode 84
Compotes 226
Coney, John 224
Connecticut 37, 41, 42, 44, 45, 80, 134, 173, 194, 224
Consol Tables 131
Conveyor 14
Cook, H. 67
Copper & Brass 48, 49
Coralene & Rubina 156
Corning 146, 152, 159, 160, 190
Cox, J. & I. 233
Cradle 52
Cree 10
Criterion 200
Cruet 234
Cupboards 84-87
Cups 149, 227
Curio Cabinet 83

Curry, John 227
Cypress 230
Cypriot Vase 161

Dakota 12
Dallin, C. E. 21
Dante 60
Davenport 88, 90
De La Cruz 225
Deans Rag Book Ltd. 244
Death Dive 15
Decanter Set 18
Decanters 150
Dedham 35
Deer 29
Deerfield 81
Desk Set 22
Desks 88-95
Desky, Donald 131
Dishes 151, 228, 229
Disney 194
Document Box 17-19
Dolls 50
Dolls' Houses 51, 168
Donald Duck Duet 245
Dore 39, 181
Dorflinger 163
Doughty, Selina 218
Dresser 87
Dressing Tables 132
Drop-Leaf Tables 133-135
Duck Decoy 24, 25
Duhme Co. 226
Dumb Waiter 114, 124
Durfee, W. H. 41

Eagle 24, 25, 27-29, 49, 169
Eagle & Eaglets 196
East Malone 246
Eastern Great Lakes 11-13
Eastern United States 54, 68, 105, 118, 144, 147, 150-157, 163, 226
Eastlake 89, 108, 119, 127
Eastman Studio 166
Edison 206-209

Elephant 26
Esso 194
Etagere 115
Exhibit Supply Co. 14

Fan 194
Favrile 23, 30, 31, 144-148, 157-161, 163, 181-185, 193
Findlay 144
Flagon 27
Flatware 230, 231
Flemington 34, 177
Floor Lamps 180, 181
Flower Bowl 147
Forbes, John W. 242
Friedrich, W. 63
Fulper Bros. 34
Fultonham 34
Fun-e-Flex 245
Furniture 52-141

Gabriel 248
Gardiner 243
Gardiner, B. 232
Gauntlets 8
Gem 203
Gilbert 45
Gillespie, Wm. 41
Glass 142-163
Glove Box 16
Goff, Washbourne & Dunn 243
'Gone With The Wind' 174, 175, 179
Goofy Gardener 244
Goose Decoy 168
Gorham 36, 179, 224, 229, 233, 237, 238, 240, 242
Grain Bin 74
Gramophone & Typewriter Co. 165, 166
Gramophones 164, 165
Great Race 15
Grueby 34, 36, 169
Guatemala 229
Gum Machine 15
Gurley, N. & L. E. 166

251

AMERICANA

Haida 12, 13
Haines Bros. 210
Hair Tonic 142
Hall Stand 112
Ham & Sam 245
Hamilton Watch Co. 47
Handel 157, 173, 176-179
Harvard 154
Hawkes 146, 152, 159, 190
Hepplewhite 54, 89, 90, 107, 136
Herzel, Paul 20
H. F. & Co. 24
Highboys 96-99
High Chair 64
Hodges Inn 223
Holland 123
Homeopathic Chest 17
Horn of Plenty 150
Horner, R. J. 53, 89
Horse Hair Singer 166
Hour Glass 154
Howard, E. 46, 47
Hubley 247
Hurd, J. 229
Hurdy-Gurdy 203
Hutch Table 126

Illinois 246
Indian 21, 23
Indian Queen 142
Indianapolis 92
Indianware 8-13
Ingraham, E. 44
Inkwell 20
Instruments 166, 167
International Mutoscope Reel Co. Ltd. 15
Ionic 44
Iron & Tin 168, 169
Ithaca 43
Ives & Co. 50

Jack in the Pulpit 156, 161
Jagging Wheel 220
Jardinieres 22, 115
Jefferson 177
252

Jensen 224, 226, 228, 230, 231, 233, 234, 240, 241
Jensen Georg 170, 225, 226, 230-232, 239, 243
Jerome 42, 44
Jewelry 170, 171
Jolly Nigger 196
Jonah and the Whale 199
Jones, Ball & Poor 233
Jugs 152, 153, 232, 233
Juke Boxes 172
Junior Monarch 165

Kalliope 201
Kataro 35
Kas 85
Kauba, Carl 22, 23
Kettle 168, 223
Keystone Comedies 211
Kirk, S. 226, 242
Kodak 166
Kutani 234

Ladder-Back Chair 64
Lanterns 186, 187
Lamp Shades 173
Lamps 174-185
Leap Frog Bank 199
Leeches 35
Leggings 9
Lemonade Jug 153
Lent, D. E. 167
Le Roux, John 229
Libby Glass 151, 159
Limbert 123, 140
Lincoln, Abraham 167, 195
Lithophane 32, 177, 222
Longcase Clocks 40, 41
Louis Marx 244, 246
Louisiana 36
Lowboys 100, 101

McDonald, Wm. F. 35
McPherson, W. J. 155
Madonna & Child 222
Maine 190
Mandarin 185
Mansard 51

Mantel Clocks 42, 43
Marble 188
Marco The Mystic 15
Marseilles 213
Martele 227
Marx, Louis 244, 246
Mary Gregory 149, 152
Mask 10, 13
Masonic 150
Massachusetts 32-36, 40, 45, 46, 56, 62, 63, 70, 71, 81, 92, 93, 95, 102, 103, 129, 130, 143, 146, 148-150, 154, 155, 158, 159, 169, 195, 219, 227, 234, 243, 248, 249
Mayflower 248
Meriden 173
Merritt 167
Michigan 123
Mickey Mouse 194, 197, 245, 247
Micmac 19
Midwife 142
Mills 15
Miniature Furniture 189
Minnie Mouse 244, 245
Minstrel Team, The 245
Mira 201
Mirrors 190-193
Moccasins 8, 11
Money Banks 196-199
Monroe, C. F. 156
Monroe, Marilyn 195
Monteith Bowl 144
Morrill, Benjamin 193
Morris Chair 62, 63
Mosher 157
Mount Washington 145, 151, 155, 156, 160, 161, 174
Music Stand 113
Musical Boxes 200, 201
Musical Jug 33
Mutoscope 15
Myer Myers 171

Nautilus 183

AMERICANA

New Bedford 155, 156, 159
New England 19, 28, 40, 56, 57, 64, 67, 68, 71, 73, 75, 76, 78-81, 84, 85, 90, 94, 97, 99, 102, 103, 106, 128, 129, 131, 133-135, 138-141, 143, 145, 149, 154, 158, 161, 168, 189
New England Glass Co. 149, 173
New Hampshire 55, 64, 72, 82, 193, 219
New Haven 44
New Jersey 177
New Melba 165
New Orleans 33
New York 18, 33, 38, 39, 45, 53, 54, 63-66, 75, 88, 89, 107, 114, 127, 141, 145-147, 152, 154, 157-161, 167, 171, 180, 183, 184, 190, 193, 205, 210, 221, 224, 227, 229, 230, 232, 233, 235, 239, 241-243, 245, 246
Newcomb 33, 36, 37
Nielsen, Harold 234
Nicholson, Leona 37
Nipper 245
Nootka 11
Norman, Maria 218
Northwood 145
Novelty Bank 196

Ohio 34, 37, 151, 226
Old Dutch 247
Oliver, Sally 219
Opera Glasses 167
Organs 202, 203
Orion 14
Owl Lifter 15

Paddles 8, 9
Paddy and the Pig 197
Paine Furniture Co. 58
Pairpoint 175, 177, 178
Paisley 213

Parfleche 9
Peacocks 234
Pedal Car 246
Pembroke Tables 137, 138
Pennsylvania 17, 19, 35, 36, 75, 82, 87, 94, 107, 137, 138, 216, 235
Pennyfarthing 247
Pepper Shaker 154
Pewter 204, 205
Pharaoh's Daughter 188
Philadelphia 18, 227, 232, 241
Phonographs 206-209
Phyfe, Duncan 63, 116
Pianos 210
Picnic Service 19
Pictures 211
Pipe Box 19
Pipe Kiln 169
Pipe Set 194
Pitkin & Brooks 144
Plains Indian 8, 10, 11
Planter 112
Plymouth 75
Pollard, William 235
Polyphon 200
Popeye Express 245
Porringer 229
Porter, Raymond 48
Portland 190
Pouch 9
Powder Jar 154
Powers, H. 188
Pram 194
Pratt, D. 40, 46
Presley, Elvis 47
Providence 233
Punch Cup 149
Punch & Judy 197-199

Quezal 145, 158
Quilts 212-217

Rattle 11, 12
Redware 32, 35
Reed & Barton 240
Regina 200, 201

Revere, Paul 33
Revere, Snr., Paul 229
Rhode Island 95, 213, 227, 230, 232, 237
Rice 33
Rochester 167
Rocking Chairs 65
Rocking Horse 246
Rogers 35
Rohde, Johan 233
Rookwood 33-37
Roxbury 41
Royal Flemish 155, 160
Roycroft 178

Salt Box 16
Samplers 218, 219
Sandwich 143, 146, 149, 150, 154, 158
Santa Claus 195
Sayre, Joel 239
Scales 166
Schoenhut 247
Scoop 26
Scorpion Fish 188
Screens 222
Scrimshaw 220, 221
Seagull 26
Secretaire Bookcases 102, 103
Sega 14
Settees 104, 107
Seward, Joshua 46
Seymour, J. & T. 130
Shaker 50, 56, 90, 135
Shaving Dish 228
Shelf 27, 32
Shepherd & Boyd 235
Sheraton 71, 94, 111, 12 112, 136
Sherman Boardman 204, 20 205
Shirayamadani 35
Shreve, Crump & Low 43, 237
Side Chairs 66-71
Sideboards 108-111
Signs 223

253

AMERICANA

Silver 224-243
Sinclaire & Co. 146
Sioux 9, 10
Sirion 201
Skillet 168
Smith Bros. 154
Sofas 104-107
South Boston Glass Co. 153
Sparkguard 48
Specimen Chest 16
Spic & Span 246
Spice Cabinet 16
Spoon Rack 18
Squire & Brother Co. 235
Stands 112-115
Steiff 246
Steinway & Son 210
Stennes, Elmer O. 45
Stereoscope 14, 166
Stern Board 29
Steuben 159, 160
Steuben, Rosaline 147
Stevens & Brown 247
Stickley Bros. 66
Stickley Gustav 54, 58, 62-66, 88, 104, 109, 111, 133, 180, 195
Stieff Co. 230
Stone 188
Stone, Anna 219
Stone, Arthur 243
Stoneware 32, 33, 36, 37
Stools 116
Stratford 177
Straus & Sons 179
Strauss, Ferdinand 245
Strongbox 17
Suites 117-122
Sunny Andy 245
Symphonion 200, 201

Tables 123-141
Tammany 196
Tavern Sign 223
Tavern Tables 138
Tea Caddy 17
Teapots 235
254

Teasets 236-241
Tea Tables 139-140
Telescope 167
Temple, Shirley 50
Terrarium 154
Tete A Tete 105
Teton 12
Texas 63
Theodolite 166
Thimble Case 234
Thomas, Seth 43, 44
Tidy Tim 244
Tiffany 20-23, 30, 31, 39, 47, 143-149, 151-155, 157-163, 171, 173, 181-185, 193-195, 224, 226, 232, 235, 239
Tin 168, 169
Tissot, M. 47
Tlingit 10, 13
Tobacconist's Sign 29
Toledo 151
Toleware 24
Tomahawk Pipe 8
Tongass 13
Totem Pole 11
Towle Silversmiths 227
Townsend, Edmund 95
Toys 244-247
Tray 155, 194, 195, 242
Trick Pony 197
Trinket Box 18
Trivet 169
Troemner, Henry 18
Tuthill 151, 155
Twenty-One 14
Typewriter 166, 167

Uncle Sam 197
United States Aviation 244
Upper Beverley 219

Valentien, A. R. 36, 37
Van Briggle Pottery 34
Vases 156-161, 243
Vermont 77, 194, 223
Victor 167
Vose & Sons 210

Walker, Izannah 50
Wall Clocks 44-46
Walley 32
Waltham 47
Wanamaker, John 234
War Eagle 15
Washington, George 49
Washstand 113-115
Watches 47
Water Barrel 204
Water Bench 112, 114
Water Cooler 35
Waterbury Clock Co. 40
Wave Crest 156
Weathervanes 248, 249
Webb 177, 178
Webb, Thomas 175
Wedding Dress 8
Weller Sicardo 34
Wells Fargo 93-95
West Virginia 157
Wheatley 32
Wheeling 144, 153, 157
Whiting Manufacturing Co. 230
Willard 45
Willard, Aaron 43
Willard, S. 41
Wilson, R. & W. 227, 232, 241
Windows 162
Windsor Chairs 72, 73
Wine Glasses 163
Winslow, Edward 228
Wolverine 245, 246
Wood & Hughes 230
Woodcock 25
Wootton Desk 92-95
Workbox 16
Work Tables 141
Wurlitzer 172, 203

Yellow Leg 28

Zilotone 246
Zodiac 14

"The world's foremost reference book on antiques."
— *The New York Times*

*The Identification and Value Guide
with more than 10,000 illustrations*

At last, an antiques price guide—updated and published annually—that can make you rich! Share the privileged information of international dealers and collectors in the priceless pages of *The Lyle Official Antiques Review* which insiders have depended on for more than a decade.

More than 600 pages cover furniture, silver, glassware, ornaments, clocks, toys, gold, bric-a-brac and much, much more—with every item precisely illustrated. Not only are the big-money auction buys here, but also the surprises you're likely to find in flea markets and antiques shops, in family garages and attics. Prices are based on actual sales records from over 150 auction houses and retail outlets in the United States and Europe. Wise buyers don't speculate about price and quality—they count on Lyle's 100 percent reliability. Follow their lead and mine the resources of *The Lyle Official Antiques Review*. It may well be the most valuable piece you'll ever invest in. *Index. Hardcover edition: $24.95. Flexible binding with jacket: $14.95.*

At your bookstore or order from Department LAV, Coward-McCann, Inc., 200 Madison Avenue, New York, NY 10016. Please add $1.60 for postage and handling to each order and state and local taxes where they apply. A complete list of all Lyle publications on antiques and of other books for collectors of antiques is available from Coward-McCann, Inc. upon request.

POCKET-SIZE IDENTIFICATION AND
PRICE GUIDES TO TWELVE CATEGORIES
OF POPULAR COLLECTIBLES

THE LYLE ANTIQUES & THEIR VALUES

GLASS • FURNITURE
SILVER • CHINA
DOLLS & TOYS • ORIENTAL ANTIQUES
ART DECO/NOUVEAU • METALWORK
KITCHENWARE
MILITARIA • AMERICANA
CLOCKS

*Each book contains over
2,000 black-and-white illustrations.*

Compiled and designed by the staff of *The Lyle Official Antiques Review,* each of these handy volumes includes up-to-the minute prices for over 2,000 items. With detailed illustrations and precise descriptions, they provide dealers, collectors, and buyers with basic information on a broadly representative selection of specialized antiques. Pocket-size and bound in a flexible cloth binding, perfect for use in shops, flea markets, and at auctions, *The Lyle Antiques and Their Values* are your keys to smart antique buying. $5.95 each.

At your bookstore or order from Department LAV, Coward-McCann, Inc., 200 Madison Avenue, New York, NY 10016. Please add $1.60 for postage and handling to each order and state and local taxes where they apply. A complete list of all Lyle publications on antiques and of other books for collectors of antiques is available from Coward-McCann, Inc. upon request.